CAREER DEVELOPMENT FOR NEW COLLEGE STUDENTS

HOW TO FIND THE RIGHT CAREER PATH AND GET
THE JOB THAT MAKES YOU HAPPY

MIKE SUN

CONTENTS

INTRODUCTION

Your success in your career will be in direct proportion to what you do after you're done what you are expected to do.

— BRIAN TRACY

On the surface, finding your ideal career path seems like a straight shot, doesn't it?

What do most people tell you?

Go to school. Work hard. Get good grades. Graduate. Get a job. Be happy.

Oh, if it were only that simple!

Navigating the waters of career development is not a linear process. In other words, there is no direct chain of events that leads from A to B to C. Choosing the right career path often involves a lengthy and sometimes messy process.

Now, more than ever, finding your footing in any given career field can be a challenge. It's never been easy to go from the classroom into the workplace. Additionally, the COVID-19 pandemic has significantly altered the landscape.

Unemployment has never been higher among young professionals. According to the US Bureau of Labor Statistics, unemployment is roughly 11.5 percent among 16- to 24-year-olds ("Employment and Unemployment among Youth Summary").

To put this figure into perspective, the overall unemployment rate in the country is 6.7 percent (Garces-Jimenez). This disproportionate unemployment rate is not slight to young people. It merely highlights the challenges young professionals have always faced.

Think about that for a minute.

Being young, in high school, college, or just out of school has always been challenging. The elusive first job has often been the gateway to a dream career path.

However, getting that first job has never been quite so easy.

How so?

Young people face many barriers when attempting to enter the workplace.

First, young professionals face a serious obstacle because they lack relevant experience. Summer jobs and paper routes do little to impress recruiters. As such, internships and volunteer gigs offer the best chance to get your foot in the door.

Second, transitioning from an internship or volunteer job into a part-time or full-time position often depends on finding the right organization and career opportunities. Usually, young professionals must start in entry-level positions that don't lead anywhere or are unrelated to their given career.

Third, career fields seem nice on paper. Kids and teens gravitate toward areas that appeal to their interests. As young people enter college, they major in career fields that suit their passions. Students talk to seasoned professionals and career counselors to better understand future job prospects—nevertheless, reality clashes with their expectations.

Unfortunately, there are times when the realities of a given profession don't mesh with expectations. For example, the bright lights of a given career obscure the toils professionals need to go through before getting to the top.

Lastly, young professionals must deal with competition. Indeed, hundreds, if not thousands, of other similar up-and-coming professionals are looking to make a name for themselves. Consequently, facing stiff competition for a limited number of job openings can discourage and demoralize even the most motivated individuals.

But it doesn't have to be that way.

Like all life's challenges, finding an appropriate path requires outside-the-box thinking. The traditional approach to career progression has become an outdated paradigm. We are now dealing with a rapidly-shifting scenario. It's as if the rug has been pulled out from under an entire generation.

This situation leaves us with two options. We can either feel resentful for the hand we've been given, or we can choose to do something about it. The first option leads down a path of negativity. This path can only breed more resentment and bitterness. Ultimately, it will never be conducive to any desired outcome. The latter option forces us to use our resources to rise above the challenge of finding our workplace niche.

You must keep your eyes open.

As educator and author Peter Drucker once said, "The best way to predict the future is to create it" (philosi-blog). Undoubtedly, we all can create our future. If we expect to follow a carefully crafted plan, we will surely fail. Moreover, there are no secret recipes or magic formulas. Finding our ideal career path is about making a concerted effort to follow our passion and look in the places we never thought to look.

This book will explore the dynamic path that leads from the classroom to the workplace. We will consider the various avenues that can take us there. Specifically, we will undertake a journey of self-discovery. This journey intends to question everything you thought you knew about yourself. Also, we will challenge our preconceived notions about what we believe to be the "right" way of building a career.

Please keep in mind that finding the sweet spot often requires letting go and allowing the universe to do its thing. There are phenomena that we can't explain. Nonetheless, fortune plays a crucial role in helping us reach the outcomes we seek.

The challenge here is to keep an open mind. In doing so, you will enable yourself to escape the rut you might be encountering. Those who think creatively have the best chance to come out ahead in uncertain times.

By the final paragraph, you will have a better sense of who you are and what you wish to achieve. Moreover, we hope you will have a clear idea of what you don't want to be. When you put both notions together, you will get a complete picture of where you're going. At the very least, you'll know where you don't want to go.

It seems the tide is beginning to turn. As the world starts to regain a sense of normalcy, we have the singular opportunity to capitalize on incoming opportunities. Companies such as PwC are now extending internship offers to approximately 12,000 people (Schwartz and Marcos). Who knows, an opportunity such as this could open the door to possibilities you may have never considered.

Let's get started with the first step to finding your right career path. We have plenty to discuss!

1

DISCOVERING WHO YOU ARE

The longest journey is the journey inward.

— DAG HAMMARSKJOLD

In today's world, all types of stimuli constantly bombard us. It seems impossible to turn off the chatter for just a moment. Indeed, finding time for thought and reflection can be quite complicated. This constant barrage of input can lead us to seek identity outside ourselves. We might think uncovering our true self requires digging through various information sources like books, documentaries, discussions, or movies. However, the journey to discover our true self begins inwardly.

Given our current social context, we must find the time to search within ourselves. That is no easy task. Consistent pressure from school, family, friends, work, and even economic and political situations can overwhelm our senses. Moreover, we may seek refuge in leisurely activities. After all, we need to do something to release all this pressure.

In this chapter, we will be taking an inward journey. We will discuss how you can understand who you are and the means we can use to get there. We will discuss how we can cut through the chatter to reveal that true inner voice.

SELF-UNDERSTANDING AND YOUR CAREER

Poet Suzy Kassem once said, "In life, most shortcuts end up taking longer than taking the longer route" (Kassem). Indeed, trying to find a shortcut to our goals may end up costing us more time than we could anticipate. When it comes to your career exploration journey, there are no shortcuts. You cannot expect to uncover the secrets to a wonderful and fulfilling career by applying some magic formula.

Your path through career exploration will take many twists and turns. There is no question that a straight line will not get you there. You see, our parents, teachers, and elders teach us that career success is a linear proposition: go to school, graduate, get a job, make money, retire, happy life.

If only it were that simple!

When you look at most successful people, their career often takes a long and winding road. They start doing one thing, go through a series of events, and eventually do what they are truly passionate about.

The longer route means that you must go through several experiences before reaching the finish line. So, if you are expecting a straight path toward your perfect career, you might be surprised by the unexpected turns along the way.

To fully grasp what this journey represents, we must first begin by understanding who we are. Without a clear understanding of our inner selves, finding a meaningful outward expression, such as our careers, may become difficult to attain.

The first step on this journey throughout your career exploration process begins with self-understanding. Understanding our innermost feelings and thoughts will lead us to become more cognizant of the goals and outcomes we wish to achieve. Self-understanding is a vital tool that will enable us to find the satisfying and fulfilling career we have always dreamed of reaching. Some go after self-understanding aggressively, while others seem to put it off as much as they can. However, most of us struggle to comprehend what "self-understanding" truly means fully.

The American Psychological Association defines self-understanding as "the attainment of knowledge about and insight into one's characteristics, including attitudes, motives, behavioral tendencies, strengths, and weaknesses. The achievement of self-understanding is one of the major goals of certain forms of psychotherapy" ("APA Dictionary of Psychology").

There are various elements to unpack in this definition. First, self-understanding involves gaining wisdom into our characteristics, attitudes, motives, behavior, and, most importantly, strengths and weaknesses. Therefore, we must be honest with ourselves. We can't afford to kid ourselves here. Please remember that you must be honest with yourself. Otherwise, it will be quite difficult to achieve true self-understanding.

Then, a practical application of self-understanding is building a solid career track. As a college student, you can relate to having trouble finding your true calling.

Think about it.

We go through our childhood receiving so-called wisdom from older or experienced individuals. Yet, many of them don't have a good sense of what their lives mean. As a result, they attempt to guide us without knowing who they are or what they aim to achieve. I am sure you know what I mean.

If we rely on others to tell us what we should do, we only find pieces of the puzzle. Therefore, we must look inward to find the complementary pieces to make the whole puzzle work.

While it may be hard to determine what you want to get out of life, it might be easier to start with what you don't want. As such, I would like to ask you to think long and hard about what you don't want to do with your life. Often, it's a much easier task than thinking about what you want.

Here is a quick and easy exercise to consider:

In a notebook, write down a list of jobs you would loathe doing. Try to picture yourself doing them and how you would feel while doing them. Try to capture a sense of what it would be like to do that job day after day, week after week.

The objective is not to depress you. Instead, the aim is to help wrap your mind around what you don't want to do. As you get a sense of what you don't want to accomplish, you can begin to understand better how you want to dedicate your time. However, you may still lack a comprehensive picture of what you truly want to achieve with your career. At this point, some outside help can greatly benefit your thought process.

THE FIVE MAIN TRAITS

As we dig deeper into our psyche, we begin to see several clear traits emerge. These traits are distinctive factors that shape who we are and what we aim to accomplish. Understanding these traits will help you get a complete picture of who are you are and where you would like to go. Moreover, knowing where you don't want to go gives you a good sense of direction as you navigate your introspection process.

The five main traits we will discuss are aptitude, achievement, interests, values, and personality. In isolation, each one of these traits reveals a crucial portion of your being. Together, they render a complete image of who you truly are. As such, we must first study them individually before putting them together (Chartrand).

Aptitude

Aptitude refers to the skills you possess in any given domain. These skills can be natural aptitudes, skills inherent to your being, and learned aptitudes. Learned aptitudes are skills we acquire as we go through life (Chartrand). We learn some skills, like language, unconsciously. As children, we don't have much control over the stimuli we receive. As a result, we learn a language as part of our natural development. However, we don't have any choice over which language we learn. That decision belongs to our parents and is subject to our environment.

As we mature, our culture places great emphasis on aptitude testing. These exams attempt to measure our skills and abilities through objective means. Since humans are naturally different, aptitude testing seeks to compare natural talent and abilities with apples-to-apples. Furthermore, aptitude testing can also measure acquired abilities such as academic skills.

The primary purpose of aptitude tests is to predict future success ("Aptitude Testing over the Years"). Consequently, the score we get on any given aptitude test serves to gauge what others can reasonably expect us to achieve. Of course, aptitude tests are not perfect; however, they are a reliable means of determining where we find ourselves compared to our peers.

Common aptitude tests include:

- Scholastic aptitude tests such as the SAT.
- General aptitude tests such as those utilized by career counselors or recruiters.
- College admissions exams include the ACT, GMAT, LSAT, or MCAT.
- Differential aptitude tests.
- Vocational exams like the Armed Services Vocational Aptitude Test.

It may surprise you to know that the military pioneered the concept of differentiated aptitudes. After all, the military has countless trades and professions available to service members. As a result, military leaders need to know their members' aptitudes to place the right people in the right places (Forgues).

Ideally, we should look at these exams as a useful tool. Aptitude tests can reveal much about your overall inclination toward one profession or another. While these tests may still leave gaps in your self-understanding, they will undoubtedly shed valuable light on your path toward complete self-understanding.

Achievement

Our achievements and accomplishments tell much about who we are.

Think about that for a moment.

In professional sports, young and up-and-coming players always get a much smaller contract than established stars.

How so?

Established stars have a track record of achievements. These athletes have won awards, delivered championships, and brought visibility to their respective sport. Athletes such as LeBron James, Tom Brady, Usain Bolt, and Michael Phelps have earned their payday. They have the medals, records, and championships to prove they are worth every penny they make.

The same goes for the rest of us. Top-tier professionals get paid the big bucks because they have a track record to prove their aptitudes. Therefore, past achievements and accomplishments are the best predictors of success (Snyderman and Rothman).

Research has shown that students who do well in academics as they develop excel in higher learning (Russo). This rationale explains why recruiters and college admissions departments emphasize good grades. After all, you cannot expect an athlete who hasn't accrued good statistics to go on to become a superstar.

Does this mean that good grades are the sole predictor of future academic success?

In short, no. However, good grades, accomplishments, awards, and recognition point toward a trend. Of course, there are instances in which an individual with little or no track record of success can produce elite-level results. While this phenomenon is possible, it's highly unlikely.

Ultimately, we should strive to do our best to accrue as many accomplishments as possible. In doing so, we can help get our foot in the door of our chosen profession.

Interests

Interests play a crucial role in shaping our professional mindset. Think about the list we made earlier. By listing the jobs you wouldn't like to do, you highlight your preferences and inclinations. Our interests help orient us as we first embark on our professional journey.

As children, we explore the professions we'd like to do one day. We hear children say, "I want to be an astronaut." But what the child truly means is, "I like science and space." We fall for the appeal of a given profession. It's that profession's underpinning that calls our attention.

To fully determine your ideal career track, you must take control of your interests. It's not enough to merely discard professions because you don't like them. Instead, meditate on why you don't like them. Here is where interest tests can help you build a more comprehensive understanding of your preferences.

Interest tests, such as occupational selection tests, offer significant insight as they correlate professions with interests. Overall, basing career assessment on interest rather than aptitude serves as a more accurate predictor of career success (Rodríguez et al.).

When you combine aptitude and interests, you get a far more precise rendering of your ideal career path. Moreover, this understanding helps you pinpoint why some careers are less appealing than others.

If possible, take a professionally conducted occupational exam. The results will help you get a solid assessment of where your interests can place you within the various jobs in your chosen field of study.

For instance, the O*NET interest profiler is a great test you can take to assess your current interests. This test is easy to use and provides an accurate assessment of your potential career track. Best of all, you can take it in the comfort of your home, residence hall, or sitting outside on a break. Take the time to do it. The investment you make in a career profile like the O*NET will pay off in droves down the line. You will find more about O*NET in the next chapter.

Values

Values often refer to personal beliefs. These beliefs show how we feel about a specific aspect of the world, society, and ourselves. For example, people with deep moral values may frown at the prospect of working in the world of finance. Nonetheless, these individuals may find greater satisfaction in the humanitarian field.

We obtain our values from various sources. They come from our parents, environment, schooling, and culture. Additionally, we can acquire or shed values as we mature. Some values may not resonate as we get older. For instance, it's common to see younger individuals gravitate more toward liberal values than older people.

As guiding principles, values are typically associated with career selection and subsequent career satisfaction (Ben-Shem and Avi-Itzhak).

In short, if you work in a profession that does not resonate with your core beliefs, you will become dissatisfied with your career choice. Conversely, when your career choice is in synch with your personal values, you can experience a greater degree of job satisfaction.

An assessment, such as Super's Work Values (Robinson and Betz), can help you see where your values fit in with your overall career picture. It is certainly worth going through this assessment to gain a solid understanding of the role your values play. Indeed, understanding your values is an integral piece of your overall career puzzle.

Personality

We cannot talk about career progression without dissecting personality. Personality is arguably the most significant factor in this equation. After all, your personality is the frame from which your whole being emerges.

Over the years, psychologists have developed quite accurate tests to gauge personality. For instance, the Myers-Briggs Test is the go-to diagnostic tool for personality assessment. This test provides you with sixteen personality types. Each type delivers a rendering of your individual traits and how they interact with other personality types (Stein and Swan). Myers-Briggs is a thorough assessment conducted by trained professionals. It is definitely worth taking as it is a significant piece of your career puzzle.

Whereas the Myers-Briggs is not the only game in town, there are other personality tests you can take. For example, the DiSC is a staple in the workplace. It contains a short series of questions that measure four main areas: dominance, influence, steadiness, and conscientiousness. These traits are crucial to career success. As such, measuring them will help you see where your strengths lie, and where you may need to improve (Rohm).

Another great test you can take is the Keirsey Temperament Sorter. This test uses a questionnaire to determine your persona based on four main archetypes: artisan, guardian, idealist, and rational. From these archetypes, you can decide which career fields fit you best. For instance, a guardian may find satisfaction in the military or law enforcement. In contrast, the rational archetype may find much more fulfillment in the STEM fields (Kelly and Jugovic).

Also, the Holland Occupational Themes test, or the Holland test, provides you with a career assessment based on six main areas. The Holland test is fairly straightforward but has proven to give accurate results. The six areas fall under the RAISEC acronym, which stands for realistic, investigative, artistic, social, enterprising, conventional. Based on your result, you can determine which areas suit you best. For instance, an artistic type would fit in well in creative fields. In contrast, an investigative type may find their true calling in research and development (Tokar and Swanson).

KICKING OFF THE JOURNEY TO SELF-UNDERSTANDING

At this point, you might be wondering where to start. You've most likely taken the SAT and other personality or vocational tests. Regardless, it might be hard to make sense of everything. You may have a load of information that somehow doesn't quite match up.

The best place to get started is with a quick and simple career interests test. This free test aims to help you get started on the road to self-understanding in your chosen career field. The test is available at:  https://www.careerhunter.io/tests/interests/take. It's free and takes roughly twenty minutes to complete. But what do you get out of it?

We've established that career interests weigh more heavily than aptitude. Naturally, it would be best if you had certain talents to do the job of your choice.

However, interests are the most important place to start. By gauging your interests, you can make an educated assessment regarding your current situation.

Here are three key elements that you will uncover:

First, you must see how your interests line up with your current professional trajectory. If they sync, you are well on your way on your journey of self-understanding. If they don't match up, you must figure out if you need to change. As such, you may choose to change your major or perhaps pursue a graduate degree in a more relevant field suited to your interests.

Second, the career interests test should reflect the list we made earlier in this chapter. It should mirror those jobs and fields you would rather avoid. In a sense, a career interests test can serve to confirm the choices you made earlier. Then, you can better comprehend what career paths mismatch with your chosen interests.

Third, you will uncover more about yourself. You will undoubtedly find aspects of your personality you may have never thought about before. Perhaps you may even discover something totally

SCAN ME

unexpected. The point is to reflect and create further introspection. This introspection process will help you better comprehend who you are and where you want to be. Ultimately, that is the main point of this book.

I would also encourage you to take other free tests, such as the free 16personalities test. This test is akin to the Myers-Briggs and can help you get a good sense of who you are. Also, this test can help you gauge who you are not. It is available at: https://www.16personalities. com/free-personality-test. The free version gives you a general overview of your personality and some specific traits. The paid version provides further insight into your test results. You choose which version you'd like to get.

Talking to a career counselor can also shed important light on your current career trajectory. Career counselors have the benefit of both training and experience. They can help point you in directions that tests cannot. For example, career counselors can share stories and anecdotes to help you reflect on your current situation. Often, counselors have the benefit of working with people just like you. As a result, they can offer valuable insights into your specific situation.

I would also like to discourage you from doing one thing. Please avoid making any sudden decisions. For instance, some students end up tossing away years of hard work by leaving school. Also, some choose to graduate and then take up jobs that are not consistent with their true values and feelings. Rash decisions are never a good idea. If anything, taking a break is useful. But please avoid making emotional decisions no matter what you do.

KEY TAKEAWAYS

Let's consider the key takeaways from this chapter.

- Self-understanding is a journey. It is an inward process in which we discover our inner selves. This process requires introspection and comprehension of what we want to achieve in life. Without introspection, it can be relatively difficult to attain true self-discovery. Also, outward stimuli are not conducive to self-understanding. As a result, looking for ourselves in the outside world doesn't yield the expected results.
- Five main traits encompass who we are. These traits fit within the Trait and Factor Theory framework. The five main traits help establish where we stand as individuals. Most importantly, the information we can distill

from each element helps us uncover more about our inner workings. Specialized tests measure each of these elements. As a result, we can gain an objective assessment of each, thereby helping us make accurate evaluations of who we are and where we hope to take our career path.

- Aptitudes are an important factor in determining our career path. Also, values and personality can serve as predictors of future success. Nevertheless, the biggest predictor of career satisfaction is interests. Interests help us determine if our chosen field of study aligns with our true inclinations. As a result, a divergence between interests and a chosen field can lead to possible job dissatisfaction or even major career pivots. Taking a career interests test can greatly help enhance our understanding of these inner inclinations.
- The best predictor of academic success is our past. Past achievements and accomplishments can help determine the likelihood of success we can expect. While good grades are not the sole means of predicting success, they do provide an accurate measure. This rationale explains why recruiters and college admissions teams place such a high

importance on academic success. Of course, there is always a possibility that underachieving individuals can hit their stride and exceed expectations.

Next Steps

Throughout this chapter, we have outlined the need for action. While the theory is pivotal, action is always the best way to go. As you gain a deeper understanding of your inner workings, you will also start to get a sense of how effective your career choices have been thus far. Consequently, it is necessary to explore the world outside of you.

The journey of self-understanding is indeed an inward process. However, the inward journey must also take you outwardly. Therefore, you must begin to transition into the outside world and explore what's out there.

Tech luminary Steve Jobs once said, "The only way to do great work is to love what you do. If you haven't found it yet, keep looking. Don't settle" (Jobs). These words resonate quite powerfully in this discussion. Sadly, we tend to settle for a given profession. For instance, we settle on what others expect us to do. Or we end up chasing the highest-paying jobs. The outcome is dissatisfaction, frustration, and a sense of emptiness. Alternatively, loving what you do fuels your

DISCOVERING WHO YOU ARE | 31

desire to keep going. This passion cultivates a fire that burns deep within.

So, what happens if you haven't found it yet?

You must keep looking. Taking the tests mentioned in this chapter is a great place to start. Now, we are going to do some more research. After taking these tests, you should have a better sense of what you would like to do. As such, you must do some digging. Ask around. Try to engage professionals who have made a career out of something you aspire to be. These professionals can provide you with insider information. From there, you can build your personal assessment of your career trajectory.

The aim at this point is to begin getting a clearer picture of what your chosen profession might look like. Things such as schedules, travel, compensation, and work-life balance are all elements you need to consider during this initial research. Once you have gathered enough information, you can determine if these jobs make sense for you.

As Steve Jobs said, "If you haven't found it yet, keep looking" (Jobs). You are at a point in your life where you can afford to take the time to think about what you want to do thoroughly. However, you cannot afford to settle. Settling at this point will cause you to set yourself back needless. This moment is the perfect time in your life to build momentum. Momentum will lead you to boost your confidence. Before you know it, your confidence will help you steer your thoughts and decisions in the right direction. You owe it to yourself to make the best decision for your current and future self.

2

EXPLORING THE WORLD
OF WORK

---

*There are no secrets to success. It is the result of
preparation, hard work, and learning from failure.*

— COLIN POWELL

U nderstanding your innermost feelings is the
first step toward your desired outcome. Indeed,
we cannot expect to get to the promised land without
surveying the path first. Therefore, we must have a
good idea of the road ahead.

In this chapter, we will take a deep dive into the world
of work. We will discuss what you can expect when you
begin testing the waters. Please bear in mind that

figuring out what's out there before making a decision will help you determine what's best for you. Ideally, you will find the right match between your interests and the jobs available to you. If possible, this match will harmonize your specific preferences with a profitable profession.

In the end, you will find a fulfilling job that can also help you make a good living. However, please don't get discouraged if you can't find something truly appealing right away. The journey through career exploration is often winding. Don't be surprised if you eventually get to your desired job field in a roundabout way. Often, we end up in our dream jobs by way of unexpected circumstances. Thus, your challenge is to recognize the right opportunities as they emerge.

Legendary race car driver Bobby Unser once said, "Success is where preparation and opportunity meet" (Brandon Reynolds). Indeed, you are now going through your preparation. By finishing school, you are preparing yourself for the right opportunities. When your preparation and those opportunities meet, you will have the winning formula you seek.

So, let's discuss how you can recognize and subsequently capitalize on those opportunities.

STARTING YOUR CAREER EXPLORATION

Your path through career exploration ought to be a thorough look at the qualities recruiters seek in candidates. In general, recruiters focus on two main areas: hard and soft skills.

Hard skills refer to all those skills that you will need to get the job done (Laker and Powell). These skills pertain to the relevant skills you need to carry out the essential functions related to your job. In other words, these are the skills you need to earn your paycheck. For instance, a computer programmer's hard skills logically include coding knowledge. Currently, there are various high in-demand hard skills. According to an Indeed survey, these are the top 20 in-demand hard skills at the moment:

1. Adaptability
2. Analysis
3. Animation
4. Artificial intelligence
5. Audio production
6. Blockchain
7. Cloud computing
8. Collaboration
9. Creativity
10. Digital journalism

11. Industrial design
12. Mobile app development
13. People management
14. Persuasion
15. Sales leadership
16. SEO/SEM marketing
17. Time management
18. Translation
19. UX design
20. Video production ("20 Skills in Demand in Today's Workforce")

As you can see, today's most demanded skills feature technology-based skills such as cloud computing, mobile app development, and artificial intelligence. Nevertheless, other non-technology-based skills such as translation, journalism, and marketing are on recruiters' radars.

The other skills on the list would constitute soft skills. But what are soft skills?

Soft skills are those nice-to-have abilities that are not essential for carrying out your job. While you could technically do your job without them, your performance would be much better if you had these skills (Robles).

Let's consider the following scenario:

A cloud computing job would naturally require knowledge and training in the cloud computing field. However, a recruiter is looking for a cloud computing expert with good leadership qualities. Technically, a candidate without good leadership qualities could do the job. However, the recruiter knows that this candidate would do a subpar job.

How so?

Suppose this job requires the candidate to manage staff. Therefore, the ideal candidate would need to combine people management skills and good leadership qualities to complement their technical expertise.

Soft skills are as important in today's business landscape as hard skills. In the Indeed survey above, we see soft skills like people management, creativity, collaboration, time management, and analysis. These skills will certainly open doors for you in any given career field.

Nevertheless, these soft skills are not the only ones you must consider.

For instance, soft skills such as emotional intelligence, interpersonal communication, and gender/racial awareness are abilities recruiters seek. Moreover, some professions require a specific set of soft skills.

Consider the service industry. Staff dealing with customers regularly must possess soft skills to bolster positive relationships with customers, business partners, and coworkers. As a result, you must be keenly aware of the specific skills your field of interest will ask you to possess. Of course, some skills may be universal (think of emotional intelligence), but other skills, such as data analysis, may be specific to your chosen career field.

You can get started with an assessment to see what skills suit you best. The free soft skills assessment test from BizLibrary will provide you with a good sense of where your soft skills are currently.  This free test is available at: https://www.bizlibrary. com/soft-skills-assessment. I would encourage you to try it out. From there, you can get a sense of where your strengths currently lie and the areas you may want to focus on moving forward.

Having a good sense of your overall skills is a great place to start. It's also crucial for you to understand how your current skills stack up against your desired career field.

LEARNING ABOUT THE WORLD OF WORK

Your career exploration cannot be complete without getting some clear insight into the world of work. You must focus on fully understanding what you need to get your foot in the door of your desired profession.

The most crucial step is knowing what information you need to find. Then, you must figure out the best place to find it. So, let's first talk about the information you need to find out.

Earlier, we discussed the importance of hard and soft skills. These skills are what you are currently developing, and employers are on the lookout for specific elements that will make you the right candidate for the job.

Here is a checklist of the information you need to research about your interested profession or job:

- Degree(s)
- Credentials
- Experience
- Hard and soft skills

Let's unpack this checklist. First, you should be aware of the degree you need for the job field you wish to pursue. Some careers don't require a four-year degree, some do, and other areas may require post-graduate studies. As such, it's essential for you to get insight into these requirements.

Next, your chosen field will require a specific set of credentials. These credentials may come in certificates, diplomas, training courses, or licenses. For instance, doctors and lawyers must have their respective licenses to practice. Therefore, you must be clear on what credentials you will need to pursue in your chosen field.

As for experience, please note that as a new college graduate, you might need to begin in entry-level positions before you can escalate to your desired position. For example, doctors start their careers as residents and gradually work their way up.

Lastly, hard and soft skills are unique to every career field. Of course, there are universal skills that everyone should have (think about good writing and communication skills). It pays to speak with professionals and recruiters about what type of skills they seek.

Let's now consider the sources of information you can turn to when seeking information about your desired career field.

There are various sources when it comes to getting occupational information. You can find information from firsthand sources, such as professionals already working in the field. Also, you can do your research by consulting documentary sources.

So, let's start with documentary sources.

The first place I encourage you to check out is the Occupational Information Network (O*NET). O*NET is the go-to database for career exploration information. As a free resource (https://www.onetonline.org), you can get started right away. O*NET allows you to search for specific occupations by typing in the related keywords. For example, suppose you're looking for information on "engineering" fields. In that case, the search will yield a breakdown of the top twenty engineering fields jobs.

Consider this result: 25-1032.00 Engineering Teachers, Postsecondary. This result shows the occupation's code and its name. If you click on the name, the site will display a summary and detailed information about the job.

Figure one shows the summary for "Engineering Teachers, Postsecondary:"

Summary Report for:
25-1032.00 - Engineering Teachers, Postsecondary

Updated 2021
Bright Outlook

Teach courses pertaining to the application of physical laws and principles of engineering for the development of machines, materials, instruments, processes, and services. Includes teachers of subjects such as chemical, civil, electrical, industrial, mechanical, mineral, and petroleum engineering. Includes both teachers primarily engaged in teaching and those who do a combination of teaching and research.

Sample of reported job titles: Assistant Professor, Associate Professor, Chemical Engineering Professor, Electrical Engineering Professor, Engineering Instructor, Engineering Professor, Environmental Engineering Professor, Instructor, Mechanical Engineering Professor, Professor

Figure 1. Summary report for "Engineering Teachers, Postsecondary."
Source: https://www.onetonline.org/link/summary/25-1032.00

As you can see, O*NET provides a highly useful overview of what a postsecondary engineering teacher can expect to encounter in this profession. Also, we can see that this job has a "Bright Outlook" tag. O*NET assigns this tag to professions that look to expand and proliferate in the short to medium term. As such, there are areas in which you will find more career opportunities moving forward.

Now, let's have a look at figure two. It shows the skills needed for a postsecondary engineering teacher.

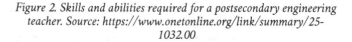

Skills

⬡ 5 of 18 displayed

○ Instructing — Teaching others how to do something
○ Learning Strategies — Selecting and using training/instructional methods and procedures appropriate for the situation when learning or teaching new things
○ Speaking — Talking to others to convey information effectively
○ Active Listening — Giving full attention to what other people are saying, taking time to understand the points being made, asking questions as appropriate, and not interrupting at inappropriate times
○ Reading Comprehension — Understanding written sentences and paragraphs in work-related documents

back to top

Abilities

⬡ 5 of 19 displayed

○ Oral Expression — The ability to communicate information and ideas in speaking so others will understand
○ Speech Clarity — The ability to speak clearly so others can understand you
○ Written Comprehension — The ability to read and understand information and ideas presented in writing
○ Oral Comprehension — The ability to listen to and understand information and ideas presented through spoken words and sentences
○ Deductive Reasoning — The ability to apply general rules to specific problems to produce answers that make sense

Figure 2. Skills and abilities required for a postsecondary engineering teacher. Source: https://www.onetonline.org/link/summary/25-1032.00

Figure two shows the combination of hard and soft skills you need to excel in this profession. Please note that we can see the top five results out of nineteen total skills and abilities. As such, it's crucial for you to go through the entire list of skills to grasp the full scope of skills and abilities related to this profession.

Also, O*NET shows the tasks associated with each profession. In figure three, we can see the tasks associated with a postsecondary engineering teacher position.

Work Activities

◯ 5 of 27 displayed

○ Thinking Creatively — Developing, designing, or creating new applications, ideas, relationships, systems, or products, including artistic contributions.
○ Training and Teaching Others — Identifying the educational needs of others, developing formal educational or training programs or classes, and teaching or instructing others.
○ Updating and Using Relevant Knowledge — Keeping up-to-date technically and applying new knowledge to your job.
○ Analyzing Data or Information — Identifying the underlying principles, reasons, or facts of information by breaking down information or data into separate parts.
○ Making Decisions and Solving Problems — Analyzing information and evaluating results to choose the best solution and solve problems.

back to top

Detailed Work Activities

◯ 5 of 29 displayed

○ Research topics in area of expertise.
○ Write articles, books or other original materials in area of expertise.
○ Develop instructional materials.
○ Evaluate student work.
○ Write grant proposals

back to top

Figure 3. Work activities associated with a postsecondary engineering teacher position. Source: https://www.onetonline.org/link/summary/ 25-1032.00

Figure three shows the top five tasks associated with a postsecondary engineering teacher position. However, twenty-seven tasks are associated with "work activities" and twenty-nine for "detailed work activities." It is advisable for you to go through these two points very carefully. Doing so will help you get a very good idea of what you can expect in this particular job. Ultimately, going through this list of activities can help you determine if this job is truly what you want to do.

Lastly, O*NET displays a section called "job zone." The job zone is a breakdown of the credentials and experience you will need in your chosen field. In keeping with our current example, figure four shows the job zone for a postsecondary engineering teacher role.

Job Zone

Title	Job Zone Five: Extensive Preparation Needed
Education	Most of these occupations require graduate school. For example, they may require a master's degree, and some require a Ph.D., M.D., or J.D. (law degree).
Related Experience	Extensive skill, knowledge, and experience are needed for these occupations. Many require more than five years of experience. For example, surgeons must complete four years of college and an additional five to seven years of specialized medical training to be able to do their job.
Job Training	Employees may need some on-the-job training, but most of these occupations assume that the person will already have the required skills, knowledge, work-related experience, and/or training.
Job Zone Examples	These occupations often involve coordinating, training, supervising, or managing the activities of others to accomplish goals. Very advanced communication and organizational skills are required. Examples include pharmacists, lawyers, astronomers, biologists, clergy, neurologists, and veterinarians.
SVP Range	(8.0 and above)

Figure 4. Job zone description for a postsecondary engineering teacher role. Source: https://www.onetonline.org/link/summary/25-1032.00

Figure four has a detailed breakdown of the credentials and qualifications you need for a postsecondary engineering teacher role. It outlines areas that need to have some experience. For instance, you will need five years of practical experience before moving into this position.

We can also see a term called "SVP range." This term stands for "Specific Vocational Preparation." It refers to the degree of preparation you need before successfully doing this job. For the position in figure four, we see an SVP range score of 8.0 out of 9.0. This score means that you need an advanced degree and four to ten years of experience (Oswald et al.). As such, this position requires a high level of preparation in various areas.

Please note that we are only scratching the surface. O*NET provides highly detailed information on every profession, including tasks, tools used, knowledge, technology skills, wages, etc. Thus, I encourage you to go through the search results thoroughly. You will find that O*NET offers extremely valuable information.

Here is a reminder: don't forget to take the O*NET interest profiler (https://www.mynextmove.org/explore/ip) in case you haven't already done so.

You can use the O*NET interest profiler to compare your interests and skills with jobs of your interest. I am sure this comparison will yield some food for thought.

SCAN ME

Suppose you are studying in Canada and interested in entering the Canadian workforce. In that case, the National Occupational Classification (NOC) system provides all the occupational information you need, just like O*NET. You can easily navigate the website (https://noc.esdc.gc.ca) by searching the job title or NOC code to learn about the primary duties, educational requirements, and other helpful information.

GETTING A FIRSTHAND PERSPECTIVE

While O*NET is a highly useful resource, it's crucial that you get firsthand information on your desired profession. Thus, talking with professionals already working in your areas of interest can be quite beneficial.

Ideally, interviewing professionals in fields of your interest will help you get a clear sense of what you can expect. Specifically, asking straightforward questions about the job requirements, tasks, compensation, and development opportunities helps to paint a clear portrait of the job itself (Gore and Hitch).

Nevertheless, finding professionals in your chosen area may be somewhat difficult at times. Therefore, I would encourage you to talk to your professors. Your professors can help put you in touch with professionals in your field of interest. Often, these professionals are already on campus. All you may need to do is make an appointment to see them.

Additionally, online communication can facilitate things. For instance, you can correspond by email or schedule video calls. The main point is to get in touch with professionals who can guide you in your exploration. I would encourage you to contact at least three professionals. In doing so, you can compare their experiences.

When contacting professionals, the following questions can help you get a good idea of the field you have in mind:

- What qualities do I need to be successful in this field?
- What credentials do I need to enter the field?
- Why did you choose this career field?
- What drew you to this career field?
- Is there anything you wish you knew before getting into this field?
- What advice would you give someone looking to enter this field?

Of course, you can ask any other questions based on your specific concerns.

Now, there's one significant concern you can bring up during an informational interview: compensation.

While some sources like O*NET provide estimated salaries, getting firsthand knowledge about salary and compensation is essential. Professionals already working in the field of your choice can give you a clear picture of how much you can make. Moreover, they can give you a sense of salary and benefit options as you progress up the ranks.

Talking to professionals can also help you get a good sense of your career path. Personal experiences are a great way for you to see firsthand how many professionals get their start in their chosen field. You will find that many don't jump right into their current occupations. Many professionals take a roundabout route to their current positions. These experiences highlight how career exploration is not a linear process. In fact, it is quite the opposite. Thus, getting direct experience from real professionals can provide you with the perspective you seek.

Overall, talking to professionals is an excellent way to get a real insight into the professional field(s) you wish to enter. Honest opinions from current industry professionals should give you plenty to consider moving forward. If anything, these opinions may change your mind. As a result, you might decide to pursue a different field. These conversations may prompt you to cross certain jobs off your list. That is perfectly fine, as it will allow you to narrow your focus until you find the right area for you.

ADDITIONAL RESOURCES FOR YOUR EXPLORATION

Getting your hands on as much information as possible as you explore career choices is critical. After all, you're making a life-altering decision. So, I'd like to offer the following resources to help you navigate the waters of your career exploration journey.

Occupational Outlook Handbook

The Occupational Outlook Handbook is a publication from the US Bureau of Labor Statistics (BLS). In this handbook, you can find the latest statistical information on every kind of occupation the BLS tracks. You can visit their website at: https://www.bls.gov/ooh/ to get access to their database.

At the BLS website, you will have easy access to labor statistics information. Specifically, you will get access to the following information:

- Median pay per occupation
- Entry-level education
- Project growth rates
- On the job training
- Projected new job creation

Indeed, this information will help you gain valuable insight into what you can expect from a given profession. Focusing on the projected growth rates and new job creation will provide you with a sense of what job opportunities you can expect in the future.

Additionally, the information you can find on median pay will help you determine if your chosen career field meets your overall expectations. After all, getting a clear idea of how much you can earn can help you make up your mind.

While browsing the Occupational Outlook Handbook on the BLS site, you will find a section titled "Browse Occupations." In this section, you can browse the information of specific occupations by going through their alphabetical index. The most enticing options lie in the buttons below.

In these buttons, you will find four very interesting options:

- Highest paying
- Fastest growing
- Most new jobs
- Field of degree

In these sections, you will find comprehensive data on jobs related to the most in -demand and highest-paying fields.

Here is a look at what you can see when you hit on the "highest paying" button:

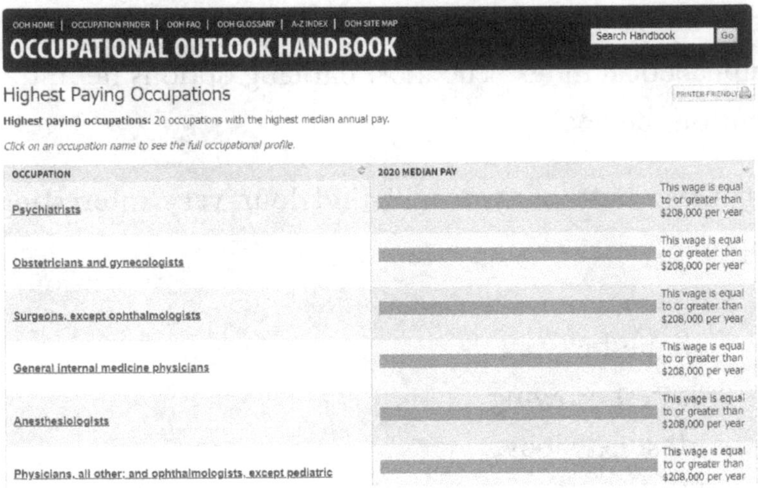

Figure 5. Highest paying occupations according to the Occupational Outlook Handbook. Source: https://www.bls.gov/ooh/highest-paying.htm

In figure five, you will find the top twenty occupations based on their highest median pay. As such, you can scroll down to the list to find which professions offer the greatest compensation. According to this list, we can see that the highest pay professions are in the medical field.

If you are keen on looking for the fastest-growing career fields, hit the "fastest-growing" button to get more information.

Figure six shows a breakdown of the fastest-growing areas according to the Occupational Outlook Handbook:

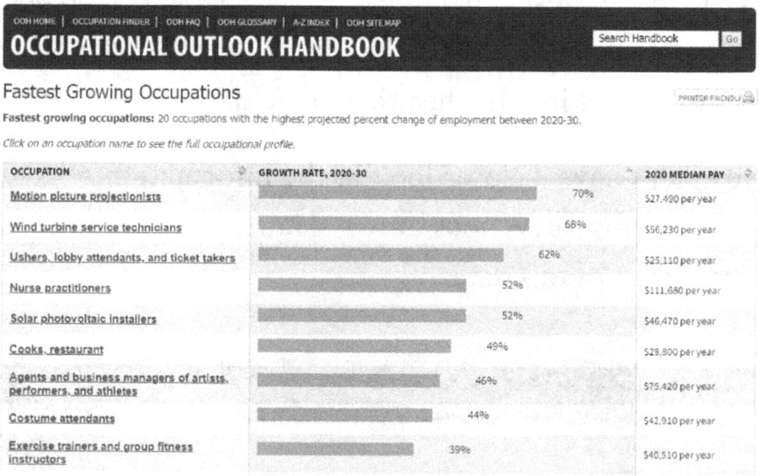
OOH HOME | OCCUPATION FINDER | OOH FAQ | OOH GLOSSARY | A-Z INDEX | OOH SITE MAP

OCCUPATIONAL OUTLOOK HANDBOOK

Search Handbook Go

Fastest Growing Occupations

PRINTER-FRIENDLY

Fastest growing occupations: 20 occupations with the highest projected percent change of employment between 2020-30.

Click on an occupation name to see the full occupational profile.

OCCUPATION	GROWTH RATE, 2020-30	2020 MEDIAN PAY
Motion picture projectionists	70%	$27,490 per year
Wind turbine service technicians	68%	$56,230 per year
Ushers, lobby attendants, and ticket takers	62%	$25,110 per year
Nurse practitioners	52%	$111,680 per year
Solar photovoltaic installers	52%	$46,470 per year
Cooks, restaurant	49%	$28,800 per year
Agents and business managers of artists, performers, and athletes	46%	$75,420 per year
Costume attendants	44%	$42,910 per year
Exercise trainers and group fitness instructors	39%	$40,510 per year

Figure 6. Fastest growing professions according to the Occupational Outlook Handbook. Source: https://www.bls.gov/ooh/fastest-growing.htm

In figure six, we see the twenty fastest growing professions. Please keep in mind that these professions don't necessarily represent the highest-paying ones. However, they represent those you can find the quickest.

While the median salary may be somewhat of a downer, remember that some professions may serve as entry-level jobs. For instance, if you're looking to become a world-class chef, working as a cook may benefit you to get valuable work experience as you go through cooking school.

Additionally, please note that nurse practitioners are fourth on the list. Their median pay is over $100,000 annually. It represents a potential avenue if you're looking to get into the health care field.

Now, let's have a closer look at the information related to the "most new jobs" area. Figure seven shows a breakdown of this data:

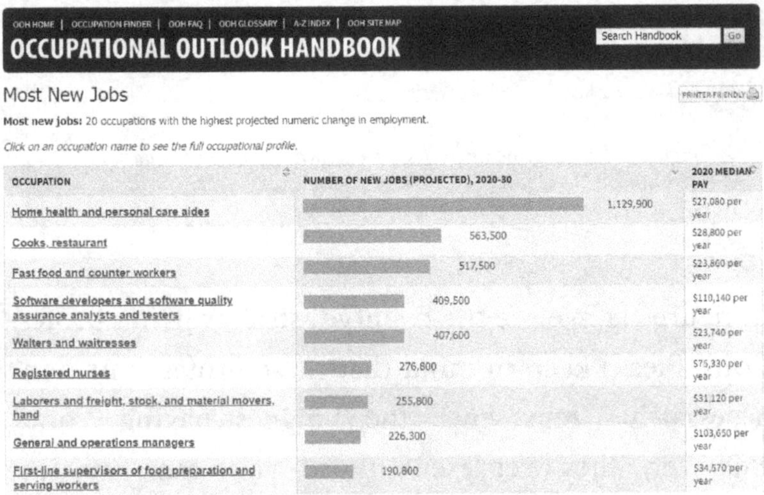
OOH HOME | OCCUPATION FINDER | OOH FAQ | OOH GLOSSARY | A-Z INDEX | OOH SITE MAP

OCCUPATIONAL OUTLOOK HANDBOOK

Search Handbook Go

Most New Jobs

PRINTER-FRIENDLY

Most new jobs: 20 occupations with the highest projected numeric change in employment.

Click on an occupation name to see the full occupational profile.

OCCUPATION	NUMBER OF NEW JOBS (PROJECTED), 2020-30	2020 MEDIAN PAY
Home health and personal care aides	1,129,900	$27,080 per year
Cooks, restaurant	563,500	$28,800 per year
Fast food and counter workers	517,500	$23,860 per year
Software developers and software quality assurance analysts and testers	409,500	$110,140 per year
Waiters and waitresses	407,600	$23,740 per year
Registered nurses	276,800	$75,330 per year
Laborers and freight, stock, and material movers, hand	255,800	$31,120 per year
General and operations managers	226,300	$103,650 per year
First-line supervisors of food preparation and serving workers	190,800	$34,570 per year

Figure 7. Fastest growing career fields according to the Occupational Outlook Handbook. Source: https://www.bls.gov/ooh/most-new-jobs.htm

Figure seven shows how "home health and personal care aides" project to add over a million jobs within the next ten years. While the median pay isn't too enticing, this field offers a great chance at snagging a job and keeping it over the next decade. If you're looking to find jobs that offer considerable growth opportunities, searching in this field will give you plenty to consider.

Online Job Review Sites

Another great source of information you can turn to is online job review sites. These sites contain information on specific jobs and companies posted by real recruiters. While O*NET or the BLS provides wonderful information, you don't get direct feedback from the professionals working on the front lines.

Job review sites can provide you with the real-life feedback you need to get.

Let's consider the most popular job review sites people turn to get real-life information.

- **Glassdoor**

Glassdoor is a highly popular site jobseekers turn to for real data. It offers a great deal of comprehensive information on jobs, compensation, and reviews. You can browse jobs by specific keywords or broad career fields. From there, you can get a good idea of what you can expect from a career field or a company.

Please keep in mind that Glassdoor is user-driven. As such, user information fuels Glassdoor's value proposition. Consequently, you should expect to see both the good and bad sides of the equation. Specifically, negative reviews can help you gain a sense of what pitfalls you may encounter.

Also, Glassdoor is an excellent tool if you are looking to get into a specific company. For instance, you can gain insight into a company before you apply. This insider perspective will help you prepare your application and be ready for a job interview when the time comes.

- **Indeed**

Indeed is most popular as a job board. It is a great place to start on any job search. But Indeed is more than a mere job board. Indeed offers user reviews on companies, jobs, pay, and working conditions. Like Glassdoor, you can expect to see both good and bad reviews. Naturally, getting this perspective will help you decide if a specific career field is right for you.

- **LinkedIn**

LinkedIn is not only a social network platform for professional connections but also a good source to search for information about specific industries and companies. Most importantly, LinkedIn is valuable for you to expose to new trends and hot topics of your interested field(s). I strongly encourage you to follow the professionals and companies you want to work for to start to engage in professional conversations.

- **Yelp**

When most people think of Yelp, they think of customer reviews. Nevertheless, you can find reviews from workers. As such, you can research specific companies within your chosen career field. These reviews tend to be very specific to companies and not industries. You may be able to see patterns within a given career field. Consequently, you can choose based on your expectations and others' experiences.

Please remember that you should take user reviews with a grain of salt. There is always the possibility that someone posted a negative review out of spite. Therefore, comparing various sites will help you get a good sense of how accurate these reviews truly are.

FINDING YOURSELF A GOOD MATCH

Now that you have ample information about virtually any job that may interest you, it's worth discussing how to match your traits, skills, goals, and experience with the job descriptions you encounter.

First, take the time to complete the assessments and reflect on "who you are," as discussed in the first chapter. If you haven't already done so, please go back to finish the first step.

Next, go through the career fields that interest you and explore "what is out there." The information will help you determine what you can expect to get out of that career. As such, you can begin to think about your professional goals with the career path this type of employment has to offer.

Consider this situation:

You aspire to become a C-level executive. Naturally, you need credentials, experience, and a proven track record. Therefore, you must look for a field that offers you this potential career path. In contrast, taking a job in the healthcare industry may limit your potential opportunities of becoming a top-level executive.

I know it might seem elementary, but plenty of students get into the wrong field because they don't have clear goals. The problem is not taking a job that doesn't match your chosen career field. The problem is that you may end up wasting precious time in a job that you would not enjoy doing or doesn't lead you where you want to go.

Yes, your dream career path is indeed a winding road. But our aim is to reduce the time needed to get you there. So, here's what I would like you to do.

Make a list of your ideal work conditions, which are goals you would like to accomplish with your career. It doesn't matter if you end up with a list of 50 items but take your traits into account. Then, take the time to whittle your list down to the work conditions you truly wish your career has. You may end up with four or five items. Once you have your list, write your goals in paragraph form. Writing out your goals in this format will help you be accountable for them. Here is what a sample paragraph might look like:

I aspire to become a C-level executive in a large, multi-national corporation. I seek to lead a team of talented individuals focused on driving innovation. I would like to earn more than $100,000 a year while helping others achieve their goals and ambitions. I will not stop until I make it to the top of my career field.

In this paragraph, we can see measurable objectives. Ideally, we want to avoid ambiguous statements like, "I want to be happy" or "I would like to make a high salary." These statements don't reflect attainable goals that you can accurately measure. After all, how can you measure a "high salary?"

Next, take your goal description and match it with job descriptions in your field of interest. For example, if you aspire to earn more than $100,000 a year, you now have a clear metric to filter jobs. From there, you can get a picture of which jobs can deliver on your desired salary expectations.

After, you must map out what it will take to get there. References such as the Occupational Outlook Handbook will provide you with the insight you need. For instance, the "financial manager" role reveals a median salary of $134,180 annually ("Financial Managers: Occupational Outlook Handbook: : U.S. Bureau of Labor Statistics").

So far, so good.

Now, let's look at what the Occupational Outlook Handbook has to say about the financial manager position:

Summary

Quick Facts: Financial Managers	
2020 Median Pay 🌐	$134,180 per year $64.51 per hour
Typical Entry-Level Education 🌐	Bachelor's degree
Work Experience in a Related Occupation 🌐	5 years or more
On-the-job Training 🌐	None
Number of Jobs, 2020 🌐	681,700
Job Outlook, 2020-30 🌐	17% (Much faster than average)
Employment Change, 2020-30 🌐	118,200

Figure 8. Summary of the financial manager position according to the Occupational Outlook Handbook. Source: https://www.bls.gov/ooh/management/financial-managers.htm

This summary shows that you need a bachelor's degree and at least five years' experience in a related field. While there is no on-the-job training, you would most likely need an advanced degree like an MBA.

So, the question is, "How can I become a financial manager?"

Fortunately, the Occupational Outlook Handbook has the answer. "Financial managers usually have experience in another business or financial occupation. For example, they may have worked as a loan officer, accountant, securities sales agent, or financial analyst" ("Financial Managers: Occupational Outlook Handbook:: U.S. Bureau of Labor Statistics").

According to this information, entry-level positions imply working in accounting, banking, or insurance. As such, I would encourage you to take the time to go over each of the descriptions for the entry-level jobs listed. In doing so, you can determine which would be a good fit for you to enter your career.

Please note that these entry-level jobs are merely steppingstones on your way to your larger goal. Please don't look at these jobs as something you have to do. Instead, look at them as valuable learning experiences.

How so?

When you become a financial manager, you will most likely have staff under your supervision. As such, you can relate to their job and what they do. As a result, you can become a truly effective financial manager because you know what your staff goes through every day.

Lastly, go over the specifics of each entry-level job. Look at the skills and experience required for each. Then, search on Glassdoor or Indeed so you can get a sense of what real-life people feel about these jobs. From there, you can talk to other people currently doing those jobs. These interactions will help you choose an entry-level position that will eventually start you on the path to your desired career.

KEY TAKEAWAYS

- Research is pivotal when it comes to finding your ideal career field. Getting accurate information on what you can expect from a given job will keep you from entering a field that may not meet your expectations. Thus, collecting information on multiple job areas will help you make the most appropriate decision based on your interests and values.
- The Occupational Outlook Handbook is the go-to source you should consult for information on any career field. It is a comprehensive guide that will support you as you navigate waters on your way to your chosen career field.
- Whenever possible, approach professors and professionals in your career field. Engaging experienced individuals will allow you to get a glimpse of what you can expect. Moreover, these insights will help you corroborate any information you can gather from the

Occupational Outlook Handbook or online searches.

- Take the time to go over your values and interests and match them with the job descriptions you find. In doing so, you can get a good idea of how well a job may line up with your expectations. This approach can help you begin narrowing your search as you contemplate testing the waters.

Next Steps

Now that you have abundant information on hand, please take the time to conduct a thorough search. Please remember that the devil is in the details. Consequently, it's important for you to get as many details as possible on your potential career path.

At this point, I would like to encourage you to keep a journal. In this journal, you can make notes on your thoughts and impressions regarding the job descriptions you encounter. These notes will allow you to keep track of your thought process. In the end, you will be able to see how your analysis has narrowed your main objective from a broad perspective to a narrower one.

Ultimately, the aim is to create a shortlist of possible jobs you would like to test out before committing to any field. In the next chapter, we will take a deep look at how you can begin testing the waters in your chosen career field. This exploration aims to help you understand what you can reasonably expect from your desired job area. So, stick around. We have lots more to talk about!

3

TIME TO TEST THE WATERS

Strategy is not a lengthy action plan. It is the evolution of a central idea through continually changing circumstances.

— JACK WELCH

Getting to know yourself in greater detail is a great first step to take in your career exploration journey. Gathering information on career areas of interest and crafting an overarching vision is a wonderful second step. But now, we must get down to business. After all, we can't expect to make our dreams come to fruition without a solid plan.

In this chapter, we will focus on the road you can expect to take on your way to your chosen career path. This chapter aims to facilitate the road as much as possible. The primary purpose is to reduce the impact that obstacles will have on your personal journey. Often, these obstacles may prove to be costly setbacks. For example, taking on a job that does not benefit your career outlook may cause you to delay your desired career track.

We will take the research and ideas from the previous chapter and translate them into a clear roadmap that you can follow. From there, we will focus on actionable steps that you can take today. These steps will allow you to narrow your search further. After all, you may still have a relatively broad scope. But that's all right. At this point, it's fine if you've narrowed down your search but haven't completely decided on the direction to take.

Hopefully, there will be a time when you can test the waters. By "testing the waters," we mean that you will have your opportunity to get your foot in the door. Often, these opportunities come in the form of entry-level positions. But we all need to start somewhere, right?

So, let's get down to business!

TESTING THE WATERS

Like Yogi Berra, we all need to try out for the team. However, it's not enough to merely make the team. You also need to play at some point. When you get the opportunity to play, you need to show that you can be a valuable team member.

As you audition for that valuable first opportunity, you will encounter various scenarios along the way. The COVID-19 pandemic has upended the current career landscape. Currently, finding the right opportunity means thinking outside the box.

A recent Forbes article listed some of the challenges that recent college grads face as they enter the workforce during the COVID-19 pandemic. Considering that most entry-level positions demand a college degree and roughly three years of relevant experience, newcomers to the workforce need to get their foot in the door somehow. The answer is going through internships (Kelly).

Indeed, the thought of graduating college without a paying gig may seem frustrating. Nevertheless, the workplace is as competitive as it's ever been. Therefore, you must be willing to explore alternatives. Internships provide you with the chance to test drive a career field before you go all in.

Think about that for a minute.

When you go through an internship, you have the chance to work a job temporarily. You can do it until your internship is up if you don't like it. Afterward, there are no hard feelings. In contrast, as you begin your career exploration, getting a full-time job may feel like a burden, particularly when you're not feeling it.

Additionally, remember that opportunities are always out there. However, they are not all right for you. As the Forbes article states, "Keep trying, stay positive, and you will eventually find the right job. Careers are marathons and not sprints. Even if you get off to a slow start, with drive and determination, you can catch up and, ultimately, win the race" (Kelly). Don't forget that you are not in a race. It doesn't matter if others cross the finish line before you do. Crossing the finish line first doesn't necessarily make you a winner. Finding the job field that truly matters to you will make you a winner. Testing the waters will give you the chance to find the right path for yourself.

HOW TO TEST YOUR CHOSEN CAREER FIELD

Testing your chosen career field boils down to getting your feet wet. Thus, you must find a way to get your foot in the door. Of course, that's easier said than done.

So, we will explore various ways you can get a good taste of what your chosen job field has to offer.

Motivational author Alan Cohen once wrote, "Do not wait until the conditions are perfect to begin. Beginning makes the conditions perfect" (Cohen).

This advice seems so apropos at this point. You see, most first-year students think they won't get an internship, much less a part-time job. So, they never try to do anything to get into their career field. This attitude causes them to put off their attempts until their second or third year. However, there's a problem with this approach.

The longer you put off getting your foot in the door, the harder it will be for you to make the best choice for your major.

Think about that for a moment.

In your first semester, it's important to connect with your academic advisor as soon as possible, who will tell you what courses you need for your major. You will likely be asked about your career goals, the length of time you hope to complete your degree studies and go over your "stumble courses." Your advisor will help you establish a realistic plan based on your scheduling needs.

Unfortunately, many students delay this discussion until the first or second year has been completed. By then, the clock is against you. You need to decide soon. That pressure can lead you to make an inappropriate choice.

Remember, it's your responsibility to reach out to your advisor. You may think it's okay to hold off because the first year is fulfilling Gen Ed requirements, but your advisor can assist you with the selection of electives that can count toward your GPA and satisfy your major's credit requirements. Delaying this discussion can hold you back one semester, hence, delaying your targeted graduation date.

Now, think about things along these lines:

Imagine you have a taste of what your ideal career field represents. You have a good idea of what you can expect from this professional area. As a result, you can confidently choose your major and, most importantly, the courses you need to take.

Doesn't that sound like a significant difference?

Don't wait until you have been in school long enough to be taken seriously. Start today on your quest for your ideal job. Let's look at ways you can get started right away.

Building Relationships through Networking

Networking is an important skill we can develop in the world of work. Specifically, networking isn't only about getting "connections." Networking is showing others what you have to offer. Perhaps you might not think you have a lot to offer now, but believe me, you have a lot to bring to the table.

In essence, networking is about building friendships and professional connections with colleagues, class-mates, friends, and those around you. As such, your goal is to surround yourself with people in the career field you wish to enter. For example, suppose you want to become a doctor. In that case, you must surround yourself with medical school professors, doctors, nurses, healthcare experts, and other medical students.

There are two main benefits you can draw from networking.

First, you gain insight and perspective when you surround yourself with like-minded people. In other words, people within your domain will help you see things as they are. For instance, doctors will provide you with insight into how hospitals work. Also, other med students can share their experiences with you. Then, you can compare your experience and see what lessons you can distill.

Second, networking allows you to stay in the loop within your profession. Often, we get tips and updates from people in specific circles. For example, you might get tips about internships or volunteering opportunities. Since many of these opportunities have limited spaces, you need to act quickly. That's where your "connections" can help you get your foot in the door.

Now, the big question is: how can you network effectively?

Business networking guru Ivan Misner once said, "Networking is more about farming than it is about hunting. It's about cultivating relationships (Misner).

Indeed, networking is about building relationships with the people around you. From there, you can begin to expand your social circle as you get more introductions.

A common misconception about networking is that you must "hunt" the right people. Once you capture those professionals, you can then sink your teeth into the opportunities you seek. However, it's tough to catch a big game when you're starting your college career. Moreover, successful networking is about playing the long game. So, please remember that your aim should be to keep as many relationships as possible around you. After all, you never know who can help you get that elusive first chance.

Ultimately, your network gets the initial entry-level positions thanks to strong character references. You see, when you don't have much experience, good character references from key people can help secure the opportunity you seek. Try your best to cultivate as many relationships as you can.

Networking is a relatively straightforward process, but you must know where to look.

A great first step you can take is fostering relationships with your professors. Your professors may seem unapproachable at first, but this isn't always the case. You can book an appointment to go over questions you may have about assignments or lectures. This interaction can allow you to see your professors outside the classroom. From there, you can seek their unique perspective on the career field you're interested in pursuing.

Please note that professors can serve as a gateway to the broader faculty. It could be that one professor can put you in touch with others who can provide you with the guidance you'd like. Moreover, you might be able to get introductions to professors at other universities who can provide you with further insights.

Building relationships with professors is a great way to gain perspective, especially if you want to get into an academic field. Nevertheless, many professors also have practical experience in the field. Therefore, your professors can provide you with valuable insights as you begin to focus on your major and your chosen career field.

Mentorships

Mentoring can become a valuable way to find your true career path. Most of us find mentors in one way or another. Sometimes, we seek them out purposely. Other times, we are fortunate to find someone who can guide us during the early stages of our careers.

Overall, a mentor is an older, more experienced individual willing to share their time, expertise, and experience. As such, younger and largely inexperienced individuals can find valuable resources in their career field.

Human resource professionals understand the value of mentoring. Often, corporations have some form of mentoring for new staff. This process involves a senior staff member coaching a new member while becoming accustomed to their new role (Megginson).

Beyond the practical approach, mentoring can build much more impactful outcomes. For instance, a 2003 study on teacher education found that mentoring helped build student teachers' skills more effectively than mere cooperative engagement. The paper titled "Mentoring as a Journey" specifically stated:

The journey involves the building of an equal relationship characterized by trust, the sharing of expertise, moral support, and knowing when to help and when to sit back" (Awaya et al.).

Let's unpack this quote. First, mentoring is about building an equal relationship. As such, your potential mentor will view you as a peer. Therefore, your mentor is not somehow superior to you. They are like you. The difference is that they have more experience and expertise than you do. Second, a mentor provides moral support. This situation implies that a successful mentoring partnership provides you with the emotional support needed on your journey. Ultimately, this moral support will become a cornerstone of your personal and professional development.

At this point, you might be thinking about how you can find a mentor.

Finding a mentor is not as hard as it might seem. Companies often have mentorship programs as part of broader corporate social responsibility endeavors. Also, professional associations often sponsor mentorship programs for college students or recent grads. For instance, the National Association of Colleges and Employers offers mentorship programs for up-and-coming students and grads in the career services or human resources field. You can find more information at: https://www.naceweb.org/about-us/get-involved/serve/mentor-program/.

Additionally, the American Association of Nurse Assessment Coordination supports a mentorship program aimed at healthcare professionals. This program supports mentorship and scholarship programs for those looking to make a career in the nursing field. You can learn more at: https://www.aapacn.org/foundation/.

To find specific professional associations in your career field, you can check out CareerOneStop. This site is a job and career exploration sponsored by the US Department of Labor. It aims to help  college students and people transitioning careers to find the best available information in any career field. Please check out: https://www.careeronestop.org/

Toolkit/Training/find-professional-associations.aspx.
Here, you will find information on professional associations in your area. Please take the time to contact them about mentorship or internship opportunities.

Virtual mentorships have become more prevalent in the past few years. Often, high-profile professionals take on a small group of college students and recent grads. These professionals offer group sessions and one-on-one coaching. You can find these opportunities through your college campus or local professional association. Also, ask around. Perhaps your professors or campus career counselors may know about them. If you can, contact your old high school counselor. They may be able to point you in the right direction.

Job Shadowing

Job shadowing is a common practice among apprentices in trades such as carpentry, plumbing, or auto mechanics. In short, job shadowing consists of an apprentice observing and participating in the activities conducted by an experienced individual. Often, apprentices serve as helpers or assistants and don't usually receive any payment. However, their learning is much more valuable than any paycheck.

In professional fields, corporations use job shadowing as part of on-the-job training. For instance, a recent grad or intern may tour every department in the company. Interns spend a few days or several weeks in each area, learning about each department's various tasks and activities. From there, interns can find the area that best fits their skills and knowledge. Additionally, the company may assign interns based on their performance.

Job shadowing is a great way for you to get a hands-on trial of how a job field works. For example, if you're interested in finance, being on the trading floor in Wall Street will help you get a feel for what stock traders go through regularly. Moreover, you'll be able to determine if this area is something you'd like to pursue.

A 2017 study showed that job undergrad students in the rehabilitation field saw an improvement in their understanding of their career field. Moreover, job shadowing allowed the participants to better link their current coursework to real-world applications in their chosen field (G. R. Oswald et al.).

Like mentorships, you can find job shadowing opportunities through professional associations. Also, professors and career counselors may know of job shadowing programs. Furthermore, local churches and community centers may serve as a hub for this type of opportunity. As always, ask around.

Volunteering

Volunteering is a straightforward way you can get hands-on experience. Often, we volunteer because we believe in a cause. However, we don't always stop to think about how volunteering can help us gain perspective on a career field.

Volunteer opportunities are plenty. You can find them through humanitarian organizations, churches, your college campus, and your local community. Programs such as Big Brothers and Big Sisters of America match children and teens with mentors in their community. For instance, a professional sports team in the Tampa, Florida, area partnered with Big Brothers and Big Sisters to help underprivileged kids find role models. Current and former players from the Tampa Rays, Buccaneers, Lightning, and Storm volunteered for the "Sports Buddies" program (MLB).

If you're interested in pursuing a career in psychology, counseling, child protection services, or social work, volunteering as a Big Brother or Big Sister can help you get the practical experience you seek. These types of programs will help you give hands-on experience while you give back to your community.

There is one other benefit to volunteering. When you volunteer, you connect with other people and organizations. As such, it is a way to further network. Thus, a volunteering opportunity may lead to interviews and potential entry-level positions or internships.

One word of caution, though. Please avoid signing up for every volunteering opportunity you find. While it might seem like a good idea, you might spread yourself too thin. As such, try your best to focus on the opportunities that will put you in touch with your specific career field.

Side Hustles and Entrepreneurship

When you hear the term "side hustle," you might get images of classmates picking up odd jobs or freelancing to make some extra money. While side hustles certainly help pay the bills, they are also a great way for you to get a feel for what jobs are truly like.

Side hustles are additional activities to your main tasks. As such, a side hustle should be something to consider in your free time, such as on the weekends, during the summer, or when you don't have a heavy course load.

Similarly, entrepreneurship can help you understand what a specific career field offers. However, entrepreneurship implies dedicating more time to that endeavor. Furthermore, you'll need to have discipline and structure. These types of projects can provide you with valuable opportunities and insight into a specific career field.

Classic examples of this concept are Bill Gates, Steve Jobs, and Mark Zuckerberg. These tech luminaries envisioned their future corporations as college students. While they eventually dropped out to pursue their passions, these examples underscore how entering the entrepreneurial field, even as a student, can help you find your true calling.

However, please proceed carefully; the last thing I want is for you to disregard your classwork. You must find a balance between your side hustles and classwork. When you find this balance, you can discover plenty of opportunities. You may even discover new ideas that you may not have considered before. If you decided to be your own boss and open a business, it would be a whole new adventure for your career. So, make sure you are ready for it!

Summer Internships and Co-op Programs

I know the thought of working through your summer break is not exactly a fun idea, but it can be a great way to get ahead of the curve. Summer internships can provide you with valuable working experience that you'll need for that elusive entry-level position.

Additionally, summer internships can yield something truly valuable: letters of recommendation, connections, and networking. Sure, it might feel like you're working for free. You might feel you're "donating" your time. However, this tradeoff is one worth considering. For instance, law students often find themselves doing paralegal work during summer breaks. Med students take on internships at clinics and hospitals to get a feel for the real thing.

College students can apply for the Reserve Officer Training Course or ROTC in the military. Perhaps the best example of summer internships in the military. College students spend their summers doing military training in ROTC instead of partying with their friends. In exchange, the military subsidizes their tuition and offers them a job when they graduate.

Similarly, cooperative education (co-op) programs or practicum as part of the academic requirement provide an experiential learning opportunity as a structured method of combining classroom-based education with practical work experience. These programs can be beneficial for students to make professional connections and have real-world experience. Many universities have partnered with companies or organizations in different industries to ensure student employment placement. Students also received salaries through most co-op programs. More than financial, the real-world experience the student gets is what makes a co-op program worth trying for.

THE RIGHT TIME TO TEST THE WATERS

The short answer is that the best time to test the waters is right now. Yes, the sooner you test the waters, the sooner you'll gain experience, insight, and information needed to make the right career choice.

On the flip side, the longer you delay, the harder it will be for you to decide on your future career path. You might find yourself taking courses that don't quite match your expectations. Moreover, you may end up getting a job you don't like. Eventually, you could pivot into another career field.

What I described is not a bad thing. However, it means you might waste precious time. If you're reading this book, it's because you're looking to maximize your time. Hence, it's crucial to explore your career field as soon as possible.

So, here's what you can do today:

Gather resources and ask around. Your professors, counselors, family, community, and even classmates might know about opportunities. If you know other classmates involved in mentorship or internship programs, ask them about these opportunities. Buy them a cup of coffee if you must. Pick their brain. Often, these interactions yield some unexpected networking.

Look up local professional associations. Make a list of those relevant to your field and plan to contact them. Find out if they have volunteering, mentorship, or internship opportunities.

ADJUSTING TO YOUR WORK ENVIRONMENT

Our environment is ever-changing. We cannot expect things to remain the same for too long. Unfortunately, we tend to cling to our comfort zone. All too often, we strive to avoid change. Nevertheless, change is an inevitable part of life. Whether we like it or not, change is always present.

Keep in mind that we must interact with our environment as individuals. As our environment changes, we must adapt to it. This concept is one of the most valuable takeaways the COVID-19 pandemic has taught us. Change happens suddenly and unexpectedly. As a result, we must do our best to adapt to it as best we can.

Consider this situation:

Before the COVID-19 pandemic, many companies were reluctant to explore work-from-home options. However, the pandemic left many companies with no choice. They had to either embrace remote working or shut down for good. The outcome was a drastic change for many workers as well. People have a work environment preference to perform their job. You would find that some workers quit their jobs and switch to fully remote or hybrid work. Nevertheless, many workers found a creative way of getting the job done.

As you test the waters of your respective field, you must be aware of how the change will be a constant throughout your career. Therefore, you must roll with the punches, so to speak. Your ability to remain in your respective career field depends on your reactions and needs to the changes in your work environment. As a result, your reactions must strive to meet the following conditions (Harper and Shoffner).

- Your relationship with your career field is an interaction between your true self and the work environment at all times. This environment includes people, material resources, organizational culture, and the physical environment itself.
- You must complete specific tasks. Thus, you must possess the abilities needed to perform these tasks.
- As long as you and your environment meet each other's needs, your relationship will continue. This correspondence will endure until circumstances change until one or the other does not meet expectations (Bayl-Smith and Griffin).
- Maintaining the correspondence between you and your environment receives the result of an individual's satisfaction. A rupture in correspondence will have an impact on satisfaction, thereby affecting career decision-making (Bayl-Smith and Griffin).
- Your job satisfaction through maintaining correspondence will result in you staying in the job. Otherwise, you will leave (Bayl-Smith and Griffin).

As you can see, as long as you maintain correspondence between you and your environment, you will remain in your career field. However, if the changing circumstance no longer meets your expectations, your satisfaction will decrease. If your satisfaction decreases significantly, you will likely leave that career field. Likewise, if you cannot adapt to the changing landscape, the correspondence with your work environment will rupture. Ultimately, your work environment will push you out of that career field.

Thus, we must be flexible and willing to adapt to change to thrive in our ever-changing professional landscape. If you fail to adapt, you may have no choice but to find a new career.

KEY TAKEAWAYS

Let's consider the key takeaways from this chapter:

- The time to test the waters is now. The longer you delay getting hands-on experience in your chosen field, the harder it will be for you to make the right choice for your career path. You may find yourself pivoting from one career to another or switching jobs frequently until you find the one that makes the most sense for you.

The main objective is to get started as soon as you can.

- Mentorships can be a valuable source of insight into your chosen field. Experience mentors can help you get a great sense of what you can expect in your selected job area. Most importantly, they have valuable expertise to share. Often, finding mentors requires some networking. Don't be afraid to reach out to professors, counselors, or even classmates. They can help you learn about mentorship opportunities. Also, reach out to your local professional associations in your field. They often sponsor mentorship programs.

- Internships and co-ops provide you with real-world experience. These opportunities can give you several weeks of continuous on-the-job learning experiences. While working through your summer may not seem overly appealing, you will find an internship offers a valuable professional experience. Furthermore, volunteering is a great way for you to learn about your ideal job area in addition to giving back to your community or supporting causes close to you.

- Keep in mind that we must be flexible and adaptable to our circumstances. By maintaining a proper correspondence between your needs and environment expectations, you can continue to be relevant in your career field. Moreover, this correspondence of yourself and the environment also leads to greater job satisfaction. Indeed, job satisfaction stems from making the right choice about your future career field. As a result, testing the waters is crucial to reveal if you truly enjoy your work.

Next Steps

There's no time like now as a first-year college student to begin your hands-on trial in your chosen career field. Please remember that you must not put off testing the waters of your ideal job area. In particular, the aim is to find out as much as you can about your chosen field before going all in.

So, here's my suggestion to you:

First, go on CareerOneStop to look for professional associations in your area. Make a list of all associations that fit the job descriptions that match your interests. From there, call, write emails, look up on LinkedIn or even visit in person to learn about possible volunteering, internships, mentorship, and any on-the-job training opportunities.

Next, contact your professors or campus career counselors. They may have information on summer internships or experiential learning opportunities. Take advantage of any possibilities you may have to get hands-on experience in your desired field. Giving up a summer may not seem pleasant now, but it will pay off later.

Finally, do your best to foster the relationships you build through any mentoring, internship, or volunteering opportunities. These "connections" can help you later to seek entry-level positions, more internship or mentoring opportunities, and provide you with valuable character references. One chance is all you need. Once you get your foot in the door, you can make a name for yourself.

In the next chapter, we will take a closer look at how you can transform these valuable ideas into a concrete action plan that will take your ideas from your mind into a tangible form. Ultimately, you will have the roadmap you need to make your ambitions come to fruition. So, stay tuned for the next chapter!

4

SET YOUR GOALS AND CREATE YOUR PATH

Curiosity keeps leading us down new paths.

— WALT DISNEY

Earlier in this journey, we crafted an overarching goal that encompassed your outcome. The purpose is to start with a big picture of your career path so that we can break it down into smaller, achievable steps.

It is essential to have a broad picture of your goals because it's easy to get lost in the big picture. It's important to focus on the smaller, actionable steps we can take to make those goals become a reality.

In this chapter, we will take a deep look at goal setting. Most importantly, we are going to focus on a clear methodology you can use to craft an effective plan. It will serve to give you a roadmap of where you intend to go. Having a clear roadmap is the best way to stay on course in these complex times. So, buckle up because we are going to take a deep dive into your career path.

SETTING EFFECTIVE GOALS

Renowned performance guru Steven Covey once said, "Begin with the end in mind" (Covey). Indeed, we are talking that advice to heart. We start from your endgame and break it down into the smaller components you need to make it happen.

Let's begin by reviewing the goal description we wrote in the previous chapter:

I aspire to become a C-level executive in a large, multinational corporation. I seek to lead a team of talented individuals focused on driving innovation. I would like to earn more than $100,000 a year while helping others achieve their goals and ambitions. I will not stop until I make it to the top of my career field.

This statement outlined a position, organization, working conditions, salary, and a main driving force. These five elements provide us with a vision that we intend to establish on our quest to find that ideal career path.

Let's break down each one of these components in greater detail.

First, let's focus on your desired position. In other words, what is your dream job? Based on the result of your self-assessment and the occupational information you learned, ask yourself what job, position, and role would make you feel like you've made it. Often, answering this question can be tricky. When you're thinking about your ideal position, avoid ambiguities such as, "I'd like to be a researcher" or "I want to work in human resources." There are many positions you could hold in any of these areas. Therefore, you must be as specific as you can. More precise statements like "I'd like to become a medical researcher focusing on cancer treatment" or "I want to work in top-level executive recruiting" narrow your focus drastically.

Next, it's important to have a good sense of what organization you'd like to join. Perhaps you're interested in working for a specific company or organization. Otherwise, think about what type of organization would make you feel fulfilled. Is it a large multinational corporation? An investment bank? A humanitarian agency? Be as specific as you can about the organization you'd like to join. Being specific will help you find an organization you can research on places like Glass-door or Indeed. For instance, if your goal is to work for Apple or Google, you can head straight to Glassdoor to see what people say about these companies.

Then, consider what your working conditions will be like. What do you expect in your work environment? Do you like interacting with people? Do you want to work from home and be independent? These consider-ations will help you get a sense of what your role looks like within your chosen organization. If you're content with playing a prominent role, you must set your sights on such a role. Alternatively, suppose you're more interested in playing a low-key role and being a front-line worker. In that case, you need to factor that into your overall assessment of future jobs.

Having a specific salary goal in mind is always good. In our example, we set a goal of $100,000. You want to set realistic expectations based on the median salary for your chosen profession. Expecting to make six figures in a career that averages half of that may be unrealistic. If your aim is to find the highest-paying job you can, it makes sense to have a specific target. Otherwise, setting your sights on the market average is a good place to start.

Last, consider what your main driving force is. Are you thinking about climbing the corporate ladder? Are you

SET YOUR GOALS AND CREATE YOUR PATH | 97

keen on making a scientific discovery? Are you focused on empowering others? Do you want to make as much money as you can? Whatever your driving force, it should be at the forefront of your objectives. Without having a clear understanding of your motivators, you may face yourself losing focus and drive. Then, redis-covering your purpose may turn into a long and arduous process. Having a clear vision now will help you avoid soul-searching down the road.

HOW TO ACHIEVE YOUR GOALS

When you think about your career goals, it's worth considering a highly effective method of attaining them. Renowned motivational speaker and time management guru Brian Tracy developed an incredibly simple yet efficient way of achieving goals. It's worked for me, so I'd like to share it with you.

Brian Tracy's popular book, "Goals!: How to Get Every-thing You Want—Faster Than You Ever Thought Possi-ble," talks about how anyone can achieve anything.

Tracy provides us with twelve steps to make our goals a reality.

Here are the twelve steps:

1. Have a Desire: What Do You Really Want?

2. Believe That Your Goal is Achievable
3. Write Your Goal Down
4. Determine Your Starting Point
5. Determine Why You Want It
6. Set a Deadline
7. Identify the Obstacles in Your Way
8. Determine the Additional Knowledge and Skills You Need
9. Determine the People Whose Help You Will Need
10. Make a Plan: Put It All Together
11. Visualize Your Goal Continually
12. Never Give Up (Tracy).

Tracy's methodology begins with having a desire. In other words, what do you really want? We have discussed this point throughout this conversation. Your interest profiler, personality tests, and aptitude assessments should all help you home in on where your true desires lie.

Next, it's crucial to have a positive mindset. As such, believing you can achieve your goals will help you get started with the tasks you need to fulfill along the way. One of those tasks is to write down your goal. Hopefully, you have already begun crafting your paragraph. If not, please take the time to start drafting some ideas.

A crucial element in making your goals a reality is setting a deadline. For instance, you can set a deadline to complete your research. While nothing is compelling you to set a specific deadline, doing so makes you accountable for your actions. As a result, holding yourself accountable will force you to follow through.

The following steps pertain to understanding the skills you need and the obstacles you may find along the way. This vital information can come from the sources we have talked about previously. However, I would encourage you to ask professionals about obstacles they encountered. I am sure you will find this information useful. Moreover, hearing about how they overcame these obstacles will be even more useful.

Consider the people you will need help from along your journey. These people should play a role, even a minor one, on your quest. Here, you will find people like teachers, coaches, mentors, family, friends, connections, and so on. So, it's your task to identify which people you need to know. For example, you may want to reach out to people in a company you're interested in joining. Knowing these professionals can help you get your foot in the door.

Perhaps the most important element from Tracy's list is the phrase, "never give up." You should never give up on your dreams. Even when things get complicated, you shouldn't drop your guard. A great way to combat disappointment is visualizing your goal become a reality. Picture yourself achieving your desired outcome. Every time you do, your mind becomes stronger. Your mind will fixate on your result. Eventually, you will develop the confidence you need to push through, especially when things get tough.

Anecdotally, visualization techniques have been shown to help promote a positive mindset among individuals. As a result, I would encourage you to take the time to visualize your success. Here is a quick exercise you can do anytime, anywhere.

- First, close your eyes and picture yourself in the position you most dream of attaining. It doesn't matter if it's your dream job or just the first entry-level position you're looking to get. Picture yourself playing the role. Imagine what you do and how you act. Most importantly, focus on your feelings, especially confidence, control, and security.
- Then, visualize your surroundings. Try to see what's around you. Think about your workplace and even the city you see.
- Once you have focused on your surroundings, look at the people you interact with regularly. Picture the people you talk to, the customers

you interact with, or the staff you supervise. Take all these things into your visualization.

- Now, open your eyes and repeat, "I will be the best ____ I can be." Please remember that success isn't about comparing yourself to anyone else. It's about becoming a better version of yourself every day. In the words of renowned psychologist Jordan B. Peterson, "Don't compare yourself with other people; compare yourself with who you were yesterday" (Peterson).

Indeed, the aim should be to outdo yourself every day. Don't worry about what others do. Go out there and focus on what's right for you. After all, your career exploration path is yours and yours alone. Everyone else has got their journey to endure. So, there is no sense in focusing on what anyone else is doing.

CRAFTING AN ACTION PLAN

Now that you have your goals firmly set in your mind, it's time to create an action plan. Legendary champion boxer Mike Tyson once remarked, "Everyone has a plan till they get punched in the mouth" (Tyson). Indeed, we all have great plans until we test them in real life. Now, I'm not suggesting you will get a punch in the mouth, but you can expect to get your fair share of metaphor-ical punches.

It's easy to craft plans in your head. These plans all make great sense until you think through them. When you sit down to analyze your suppositions, you begin to see holes in them. That's what we are looking to accomplish here. We want to find as many holes as we can. In doing so, we can better understand where potential pitfalls may lie.

Consider this situation:

You plan to become a doctor. So, what's the plan? Get an undergrad degree, go to medical school, do your residency, graduate, get a job, sail off into the sunset.

That sounds like a plan, doesn't it?

However, have you thought about the potential pitfalls you may encounter?

A common issue among medical students is mistreat-ment. Unfortunately, prolonged exposure to mistreat-ment eventually leads to burnout (Dyrbye et al.).

One study reported that a little more than 75 percent of participants reported some type of mistreatment from faculty or staff members (Cook et al.).

Now, I am not making this point to discourage you from going to medical school. I am merely trying to point out that you will take punches along the way. Therefore, your action plan needs to account for these proverbial punches. If you're not prepared for them, at least mentally, how can you be sure you'll have the grit to get through the entire journey?

When crafting your action plan, it's important to map out what you perceive to be the road ahead while considering the potential bumps you will encounter. Thus, we are going to take a page out of Brian Tracy's playbook while adding our signature on the plan itself.

What Is an Action Plan?

An action plan consists of breaking down the tasks needed to accomplish a goal. You can reduce most objectives into smaller, intermediate tasks. When you put the smaller tasks together, you can build the larger task, thereby achieving your goal.

Initially, it's important for you to take the big picture goal you plan to achieve and break it down into smaller steps you'll need to get through first.

Let's consider this situation:

Aspiring chefs don't often go from cooking school straight into an executive chef position. Top-tier chefs generally must pay their dues by going through various jobs to build experience. For example, would-be chefs start as kitchen staff, move on to prep cooks, cooks, then become sous-chefs, and eventually executive chefs. Of course, this process is not immutable. Nevertheless, it serves to highlight how you can take an overarching goal and break it down into smaller, more manageable chunks.

The biggest benefit of seeing your goal in smaller chunks is simplifying the process. When you visualize your goals as one large goal, you may run out of steam before making any significant headway. This reason highlights the mantra marathon runners use to keep themselves going: "One mile at a time." If you think about running 26 miles, you may not even get through the first half of the race. In contrast, focusing on the first mile, then the next one, and the next, and the next until you reach the finish line, will make it much easier for you to finish the race.

Legendary motivational speaker Tony Robbins once said, "Setting goals is the first step in turning the invisible into the visible" (Robbins).

At the moment, your dream career path may be invisible. After all, it's in your head. It's in your heart. What we want is to take these unseen contents in your heart and transform them into tangible evidence of your success.

WRITING AN ACTION PLAN IN FIVE STEPS

Writing an action plan doesn't have to be a laborious process. In fact, writing an action plan is about being concise and precise. Drafting a voluminous plan will do little to help you achieve your goals.

Yankees Hall of Fame catcher Yogi Berra once imparted this wisdom, "Without a plan, even the most brilliant business can get lost. You need to have goals, create milestones and have a strategy in place to set yourself up for success" (Berra).

Take Yogi's word for it. He won thirteen World Series Championships with the New York Yankees. He also won three American League Most Valuable Player awards (admin).

Does that kind of success happen by accident?

Not likely. Yogi Berra knew that he had to work his way up. He tried out for the St. Louis Cardinals and received an offer to join the team. He declined the offer to pursue other try out opportunities. Ultimately, he signed with the New York Yankees in 1942. Yogi played in the minor leagues until he got his first chance at the Big Leagues in 1946. From 1947 until his retirement in 1963, Yogi cemented his standing as one of the all-time greats in baseball (admin).

His success was possible thanks to his determination and dedication to excel at every step of the process.

Yogi Berra's story underscores the need to have a clear roadmap for your career. All you need is to get that first chance to show what you can do. That first chance begins with your action plan.

The methodology I propose herein consists of five steps. Each step builds on the previous one. When you put the entire plan together, you can articulate a vision for your career plan. Although there is one word of caution here, plans are flexible. In other words, they are not cast in stone. This situation means that you must also be willing to alter your plans as circumstances around you change.

Let's now look at the five major steps:

1. Write SMART goals
2. Draft a To-Do list
3. Establish deadlines

4. Assign resources

5. Track progress

These steps serve an individual purpose. Therefore, it is crucial for you to follow them sequentially. In doing so, you'll create a coherent process you can easily tweak if need be. Otherwise, skipping steps or planning them out of order may confuse you. As such, we will discuss these steps one by one.

Write SMART goals

SMART goals refer to a method for articulating specific actions you intend to accomplish. SMART is an acronym that stands for:

- Specific
- Measurable
- Attainable
- Relevant
- Time-based

When thinking about your action plan, think about the underlying actions along with SMART terms. When goals are specific, you outline exactly what you intend to do. Goals should be measurable to determine precisely when you have achieved them. Also, actions must be attainable. In other words, these are the actions you can truly accomplish.

Moreover, these actions should be relevant to your overall plan. Time-based goals imply setting a deadline. This deadline needs to be realistic. Please note that goals without a deadline often go unfulfilled.

The SMART method will help you establish realistic actions that will help you achieve your outcome. Consider this example:

- Specific: I will get a teaching assistant job in my city.
- Measurable: I will send out five applications per week.
- Attainable: I will focus on teaching assistant positions that don't require an advanced degree.
- Relevant: I will focus on a teaching assistant position that can lead me to get a full-time teaching position.
- Time-based: I will get a teaching assistant position within six months.

In this example, our focus is on getting a teaching assistant position that will lead to a full-time position. As such, starting as an assistant is an intermediate step on the way to the goal. Most importantly, this goal will be possible within six months.

Draft a To-Do list

Writing great goals is a perfect way to start your action plan. Nevertheless, writing goals doesn't accomplish much until you complete real tasks. At this point, a To-Do list can help you make sense of what activities you can do to help you advance your objectives.

Now, there's a specific trick to making an effective To-Do list. You must figure out how each task links to the next. From there, you can determine which tasks are relevant to your overall goal.

Consider this situation:

You want to become a research assistant. As such, you break down this goal into smaller tasks. To visualize the tasks, you craft a list.

- Gather information on available opportunities (online search)
- Visit labs located on campus
- Talk to professors
- Ask current lab assistants about opportunities
- Send applications
- Follow up applications

In this list, the tasks specifically help you achieve that research assistant position you seek. While this list is obvious, it has one significant benefit. Writing things down makes you accountable to yourself. Having your plans in black and white forces you to follow through. Looking at a list of incomplete tasks is a great way of keeping your mind focused on what you should do instead of using your time on irrelevant tasks.

Establish Deadlines

The perfect follow-up to a To-Do list is setting a timeline for each goal. Once again, the aim is to hold yourself accountable for these tasks' completion. Without clear deadlines, it may be difficult for you to follow through.

Let's look at the To-Do list from the previous exercise, but now we will attach a timeline to it:

- Gather information on available opportunities (online search) – Monday
- Visit labs located on campus – Tuesday and Wednesday
- Talk to professors – next Monday
- Ask current lab assistants about opportunities – Friday
- Send applications – weekend
- Follow up applications – next week

As you can see, adding a deadline to your tasks makes a huge difference. While these deadlines are not necessarily unchangeable, they serve to keep your mind focused on completing them. Keep in mind that accountability is a crucial factor in ensuring that you will follow through on your goals.

Assign Resources

When you assign resources, you establish what elements you need to achieve a goal. There are occasions when you need material resources like objects or perhaps money. There are other times when the resources you need are people.

In the previous list, the resource you need to consider is people. Contacting the right people will help you get that research assistant position. For example, you will need to contact your professors, classmates, neighbors, community members, practically anyone that can help you connect with opportunity you seek.

Also, don't neglect to assign time to your tasks. Often, we fail to accomplish our tasks because we don't dedicate enough time to them. Therefore, make sure you clear enough time on your schedule to ensure you can call, visit, and write people you want to connect with. Furthermore, please ensure you set aside time to follow up. You may need to clear one morning or afternoon to make phone calls and write emails. In other cases, you may need to pluck away an hour here and there to make sure you reach the people you want to achieve.

Track Progress

We often overlook the importance of tracking progress. There are times when we merely write up a To-Do list but don't have any meaningful way of monitoring progress. As a result, we can't be entirely sure about how much headway we make.

In our example, you can track progress by making a checklist of the people you need to contact. Checking names off a list is a good way of knowing who you've contacted and who you still need to reach. Additionally, flagging people's names for follow-up emails is a great way to help you track your progress.

Here is a trick I use to help me keep track of my progress. It's simple but effective. I use reminders on my phone to help me keep track of things I need to do and the people I need to contact. Set up your reminders based on your current availability and schedule. When you have set time aside, leave yourself a reminder so you don't spend your time on something else. Using automated technology to help you free up valuable brainpower for the activities that truly matter.

KEY TAKEAWAYS

Let's consider the key takeaways from this chapter:

- Setting effective goals is the backbone of your career exploration. While self-knowledge will serve as a guiding beacon, setting effective goals will help you have a keen understanding of where you're going. Thus, you must have a clear picture of your overarching goal. This will provide you with the vision you need to stay the course.
- Your goals, as effective as they may be, need an equally effective action plan. Your action plan should focus on realistic outcomes. Of course, there is nothing wrong with being ambitious. However, your ambition may lead you to set unattainable or unrealistic goals. Ultimately, your inability to achieve your aspirations may cause frustration and disappointment. Naturally, these feelings are something we must avoid whenever possible.
- Setting deadlines and assigning resources to the tasks in your action plan will help keep you accountable. Holding yourself accountable for your goals will help you achieve them. Otherwise, you may lose focus and motivation.

You don't need anyone to pressure you. Having a clear vision will help you stay true to your purpose.

- We must be willing to adapt to the changing circumstances around us. Change is a constant in the workplace. As the COVID-19 pandemic has shown us, changes can happen unexpectedly and in short order. As such, your ability to adjust to your environment will help maintain the correspondence between you and your environment, so don't be afraid to think outside the box. Often, finding creative solutions to the situations around you can help you find the right path for you to reach your ambitions.

Next Steps

Take the time to work on your action plan. I know that it's not always easy to write down goals and draft an action plan. There are occasions when you need to give yourself time to think things through. However, taking time out to do soul-searching isn't always possible.

So, here's something I would like you to consider:

Whenever you can take some time off your current situation, go away somewhere for a weekend. You don't need to go far. The idea is to spend some time alone in a place where you can relax and recalibrate. During this time, write your main objective. Take the time to carefully think about what you want to achieve with your career.

Once you have written your goal, get started on your action plan. You don't have to finish it in one sitting. You may only come away with a rough sketch of your action plan. But once you have it, you can fine-tune it later. Make time to work on your action plan until you have a reasonable roadmap for your career ambitions.

Start making some key decisions. For instance, assign resources such as time to the tasks in your action plan. Start making phone calls, collecting information, or visiting places. Test the waters as soon as you can. In doing so, you'll get a better sense of direction. You will quickly realize if the path you're on is the right one for you. Otherwise, don't be afraid to make adjustments. You can always adjust your plan but not your goals.

In the next chapter, we will explore how you can showcase your skills through effective techniques to highlight what you bring to the table. Please note that impressions are important. So, it's vital to ensure that you put your best foot forward when you go down your ideal career path.

5

GET READY TO SHOWCASE YOURSELF

You never get a second chance to make a first impression.

— WILL ROGERS

When you plan to start down your career path, and you are ready to test the waters, you must get ready to face prospective recruiters, admissions boards, and various organizations. As such, it's essential to put your best foot forward.

First impressions play a crucial role in helping you get your foot in the door. Good applications will aid you in making your action plan become a reality. Making a good first impression is important as you make a name for yourself. Over time, your track record will speak for itself. But in the meantime, you must ensure that you always put your best foot forward.

In this chapter, we will take a closer look at how you can leverage a good application to help you showcase the skillset you bring to the table. Moreover, we are going to discuss effective ways and techniques you can use to put your best foot forward every step of the way.

PUTTING YOUR CV AND RESUME TOGETHER

Most students confuse a CV (curriculum vitae) with a resume. While they generally serve the same function, they have distinct purposes.

The Cambridge dictionary defines a CV as a "short written description of your education, qualifications, previous job experiences, and sometimes also your personal interests, that you send to an employer when you are trying to get a job" (Cambridge Dictionary CV). Thus, a CV is a summary to describe yourself, including achievements, qualifications, and experience with the purpose of seeking employment.

A resume has a similar definition. The Cambridge dictionary states that it is "a written statement of your educational and work experience" (Cambridge Dictionary, "Resume"). A resume provides prospective employers with an overview of your academic credentials and experience.

So, what's the difference?

The CV shows a complete history of your career and credentials in linear order. The length of the document is variable ("Curriculum Vitae - Definition, What to Include, and How to Format").

A CV summarizes your overall relevant information; it could be longer to include publications, professional training and other achievements. If you are applying for a position in post-secondary education, you need to prepare an academic CV. There are no page limits for your academic CV as it will become longer and longer as your career progresses in higher education. In contrast, a resume presents a concise picture of your skills and qualifications for a specific position, so length tends to be shorter (generally 1-2 pages).

What essential information should you need to include on your resume/CV? Including too much information may become a distraction. Too little information will not do you any good.

To find that sweet spot, let's consider some guidelines for writing your CV or resume:

1. Your resume/CV must be relevant to the position you're applying for and the organization you're contacting. A cookie-cutter resume/CV won't cut it. While you may have skills that apply to various jobs and organizations, each application has its set of requirements. Therefore, you must ensure that your resume/CV reflects the requirements for that specific application.

2. Avoid bending the truth. Unfortunately, many students try to get away with embellishing their experiences or providing misleading information about their credentials. It is only a question of time before the truth comes out. Naturally, honesty is always the best policy.

3. Include a personal headline or statement to highlight why you are the right person for the position. Personal statements generally consist of three or four sentences explaining why you are qualified for the position. This statement should compel anyone reading your resume/CV to look past the first few lines.

4. Use keywords relevant to the position(s) you seek. This tip is crucial when uploading your

resume/CV to job sites or online portals. These sites use algorithms to detect specific applications. As such, you want to make sure you include relevant keywords as much as possible. For instance, if you're applying for a "teaching assistant" position, be sure to include "teaching," "teacher," or "assistant" as many times as is reasonable in your resume.

5. Also, please ensure your resume looks good. This tip applies to ensuring the font and layout look neat and easily readable. Also, make sure there are no typos or grammatical errors. Being sloppy with your resume/CV sends a terrible message.

6. And be sure to update your resume/CV as often as you need to. A good rule of thumb is to freshen your resume/CV every couple of months. Go over it and make sure to change or update anything necessary.

Additionally, copying and pasting information from your resume/CV can save you time if you're filling out online applications. However, always ensure that the information you're inputting is relevant to the organization and position. Blindly copying and pasting may end up being counterproductive.

CHOOSING BETWEEN A CV AND A RESUME

Overall, a CV and a resume are essentially the same. We have established that a CV is longer than a resume. You may be wondering if you should create a CV, resume, or both. The short answer is that you should write both; however, the long answer requires a bit more consideration.

First, a CV is longer and includes various sections. Therefore, I suggest that you begin crafting your CV based on the model we will discuss shortly. It is the best way to map out your overall career history and review what you have accomplished in the past. However, you may find it challenging to fill out some sections. For instance, sections on academic publications and professional associations may be blank at this point.

Second, a resume is shorter and provides a precise summary of your skillset and qualification for a specific position. Thus, a resume is your best choice at this point if you start testing the water in your chosen field to accumulate relevant experiences. Highlighting your relevant experiences and qualifications is the best way to showcase your talents and get the job.

Third, please remember that a CV is an evolving document. As you obtain more achievements, you can populate your CV. Your CV will always be a work in progress. As a result, use your resume as a condensed form of your CV. You can always submit your CV whenever organizations require a more elaborate summary of your history.

Remember that older professionals with completed degrees, publications, achievements, and broader work history prefer a CV. Avoid trying to compete with others. Don't worry if your CV is short at this point. Eventually, you will have a significant number of items to include.

Ultimately, your CV or resume is the best tool you can use to make a solid first impression. So, please make sure you use it to put your best foot forward.

THINGS TO INCLUDE IN A CV

When crafting your CV, you may not know what to include. So, let's look at the information you can consider.

- **Headline**. A headline is a statement that describes why you are the right person and what you bring to the table. A great statement is short and sweet. A straightforward sentence will help get your point across. For instance, "Highly Motivated Team Player Looking for an

Opportunity To Excel in the Academic Research Field" is a great way to headline who you are and what you're looking to accomplish.

- **Profile**. A profile goes atop your CV. As with a headline, you can use a personal profile to showcase yourself. Here is a great example of a profile as a new college student, "Class valedictorian currently attending freshman year. Has demonstrated a keen interest in engineering and chemistry. Able to conduct dedicated research and statistical analysis. Willing to work under pressure in complex projects." In this profile, we see a personal accomplishment and a clear character description.

- **Personal information**. The big question is how much information is too much? The fact is that you should only include relevant information such as your name, contact information (phone number and email), and the city and state you currently reside. Additionally, other information such as gender, marital status, and age is completely optional. I would encourage you to leave any personal identity information off to avoid biases. You can always furnish whatever information you need to submit later.

- **Education**. Ideally, your education should list

your degrees and relevant certificates. Since you may not have too many of those at this point, you can start by listing your current course of study. Also, listing your high school and any other relevant courses and certificates would help. For instance, if you've done first-aid training, you could include that to bolster your chances in the healthcare field. However, if you're applying for a finance position, a first-aid course may not be the best idea, so be selective.

- **Work experience.** This area may be tricky. You may not have too much experience to speak of. Consider adding your practicums part-time work, volunteering, student leadership experience, and campus activities into this section. You can also include any other instances you've assisted professors or high school teachers.

- **Skills.** In this section, you can list all the relevant skills you possess. These skills may include computer skills, languages, or any other training. Please ensure they are relevant to the application you're submitting.

- **Honors and awards.** Here, you can list any significant achievements. For example, you can list awards for high grades, recommendations from teachers and professors, or contests and competitions you have won. This section is a great opportunity to list any athletic achievements you may have.

- **Publications and presentations.** This section should include any written pieces you have published or presentations you have delivered. You can include speeches given at your church, local community groups, or student organizations. Also, suppose you have a blog or have contributed to a student newspaper. In that case, you can certainly include that in this section.

- **Professional memberships.** Memberships to professional associations can include all sorts of associations. For instance, if you're a Scout, a member of a religious organization, charity, or some other kind of society, you can list that here. This section can help frame your character, thereby providing an image of your overall persona.

As you can see, a CV can become quite extensive. Try your best to keep it between two to three pages. Once you have a good working draft, you can condense it into a single-page resume. You should include the most relevant information from the areas indicated above on this single page. Please note that your resume does not need to have every section. Mainly, your personal information, education, and work history, along with significant honors, achievements, and memberships, should suffice.

At this point, you should be ready to start building your CV and resume. However, it may be somewhat complicated when choosing a format, font, style, and so on. Free resume building at resume.com is a great tool you can use to build your resume quickly and easily. Also, Microsoft Word has some nice templates you can use. I would encourage you to try out various formats to see which you prefer.

THINKING OUTSIDE THE BOX WITH MODERN RESUMES

Looking for hiring trends, TikTok launched its resume feature in summer 2021. More and more companies and organizations are thinking outside the box with their recruiting practices. Candidates are letting their creative juices flow to stand out among the crowd.

That's where modern resumes come into play.

Of course, traditional resumes are highly effective. When done right, a traditional resume can provide recruiters and admissions professionals a clear picture of who you are. But competition is fierce, so any competitive advantage you can get goes a long way toward helping you land that first golden opportunity.

So, what exactly is a modern resume?

In short, a modern resume is any resume or CV type that does not employ the conventional format we have discussed. Consequently, modern resumes use formats like video, slideshows, timelines, or animated presentations. Now, please keep in mind we're not talking about putting on a dog and pony show. We're talking about showcasing your skillset in a creative manner.

Let's look at the various formats you can employ for a modern resume.

Video resumes

Indeed, TikTok short video resumes are "it" right now. Video resumes provide a great alternative to a standard resume or CV format. They allow recruiters and admissions officers to see the real you in action.

Here is an excellent TikTok resume https://www.tiktok.com/@ jadecarsonxo/video/ 6982257372798455046? sender_device=pc& sender_web_id=

7044284302466008581&is_from_webapp=v1&
is_copy_url=0.

A TikTok resume isn't a single video resume style you can follow. There are various formats you can use. Here are some examples of the most creative video resume styles:

- **Animation**. Animation videos may seem cartoonish but can certainly help capture people's attention, especially if you're in a creative field. This is a nice example of an animation video resume: https://www.youtube.com/watch?v=SbjAZwt27AY.

SCAN ME

- **Whiteboard**. Whiteboard videos are common when explaining concepts or ideas. These videos allow you to present various pieces of information in a seamless flow. Whiteboard videos can make a great video resume, especially if you want to highlight various aspects of your personal, academic, and professional life. Here is a great example: https://youtu.be/OdR1H1BiB-M.

SCAN ME

- **Stop motion**. Stop motion videos are a highly creative way of summarizing the main points of your CV or resume. You can easily use this format to run through the highlights while focusing on the specific information you want to emphasize. This is a wonderful example: https://www.youtube.com/watch?v=yKw9IgTngUI.

SCAN ME

The examples above can truly make your resume stand out. You can always point the camera at yourself and speak. Often, looking presentable in front of the camera and speaking clearly can make a lasting impression. You can shoot a wonderful video using your cellphone or laptop camera. Preferably, choosing a nice background in a quiet spot will make your voice stand out. Ultimately, recruiters and admissions officers want to see the real you. What could be better than your voice in real-time?

Tips for a Successful Video Resume

A successful video resume, regardless of format, should contain the following elements:

- Introduction
- Selling point
- Call to action

Let's take a closer look at each element.

- **Introduction.** Your introduction should be no more than a few seconds. Introductions are about conveying confidence as you make a good first impression. Most importantly, your introduction should state your intentions. For instance:

"Hello, this is _____ and I'm a hardworking, outgoing, chemistry major looking to build a career in pharmaceutical research."

- **Selling point.** Your selling point refers to your specific skillset, experience, and qualifications. It doesn't matter if you don't have an extensive list of achievements. The important thing is to give viewers a clear idea of who you are. Also, don't forget to include keywords from the job description. For example:

"I'm a third-year student currently focusing on biochemistry. I've volunteered as a research assistant in the campus lab. I've assisted graduate students with their research for masters and doctoral dissertations. I'm committed to doing my best to provide useful support and learn as much as I can."

- **Call to action.** Your call to action should encapsulate your strong points and leave the door open for the viewer to contact you. Ultimately, your call to action is about delivering a strong and memorable closing. For instance:

"Thank you for taking the time to watch my video resume. I'm confident I can be a valuable member of your organization. I have the skillset, determination, and work ethic to make a difference. Please don't hesitate to contact me. I'll be looking forward to hearing from you soon."

Overall, your video resume should be somewhere between one to three minutes. Please remember that recruiters and admissions officers are busy people, and you want to save them as much time as you can.

Slideshow Resumes

A slideshow resume allows recruiters to peruse your resume easily without having to read a text-heavy document. Using a slideshow greatly enhances your information's visibility. For instance, you can assign one slide per section of your resume. You can organize your slideshow resume as follows:

- Personal information
- Educational background
- Work/volunteer experience
- Qualifications and skills
- Contact information

Your slideshow resume can easily become four or five slides. Most importantly, please ensure they are not loaded with text. Loading slides with text makes it harder for people to read.

Also, using images with information in bullet points helps viewers find your information quickly and easily. Here are some tips to consider:

- Use bright templates and backgrounds.
- Avoid text-heavy slides.
- Keep images simple. It's best to avoid visual overload.
- Highlight main points.

- Above all, keep it short and sweet.

Uploading your slideshow resume on SlideShare is a great way to make it freely available. Also, creating a PowerPoint presentation can facilitate emailing and uploading to online platforms. Check out this wonderful example on SlideShare https://www.slideshare.net/jeremybaker/jeremy-bakers-visual-resume-1216240.

Timeline Resumes

Timeline resumes, as the name suggests, use a horizontal format to present relevant educational and work information. This format streamlines your entire history in a quick and easily digestible format.

Producing a timeline resume requires you to organize your information in chronological order. As a result, you're placing greater emphasis on when things happened. This format could be a great option if you're looking to highlight specific achievements and events in your life.

Here are some tips for producing timeline resumes:

- Avoid overloading your timeline. Fill the timeline with relevant information and events.
- Ensure to keep your timeline consistent. Leaving large gaps and filling in multiple events in a short period may seem odd.
- Make sure the timeline is legible. Cramming too much information can lead to your timeline seeming overcrowded and hard to read.
- Horizontal timelines work better than vertical ones.

You can use Microsoft Word, Excel, or PowerPoint templates to produce your timeline. However, presenting it in PDF format helps people view it easily. Also, sharing your timeline

SCAN ME

resume as an image file is a good idea. You can also upload it to SlideShare or keep it on your LinkedIn profile for easy access.

Check out these great Microsoft Office templates to help you build your timeline resume https://templates. office.com/en-in/resume-timeline-tm00002080.

Another essential component of your application is your cover letter. Let's look at your cover letter.

ALL ABOUT COVER LETTERS

When applying for a job, internship, volunteering opportunity, or scholarship, you need to include a cover letter with your application. A cover letter is hugely significant as it is generally sent along with your resume to prospective employers. As such, a good cover letter can boost your chance of getting a call for an interview (Kagan).

Please keep in mind that cover letters have become more important in recent years due to increased online applications. Therefore, organizations generally ask applicants to upload their resumes and cover letters. After, organizations may request additional documentation. This request is usually part of an onboarding process.

A cover letter's main purpose is to highlight why you're the right person for a position. Thus, you must expand on the main reasons and qualifications for your application. Moreover, a cover letter allows you to express your interest in the position you want. A great cover letter gives you the chance to distinguish yourself from your competition. As a result, you must tailor your cover letter for each application you submit. Cookie-cutter cover letters won't get you very far. Recruiters will see through them. So, please take the time to consider a fresh cover letter every time you apply carefully.

TIPS FOR AN OUTSTANDING COVER LETTER

A poor cover letter can derail a great application. After all, most recruiters spend less than a couple of minutes per application. Thus, a solid cover letter will get you past the first filter. As a result, your cover letter should serve as a calling card for an interview. Here are some tips to help you write an effective cover letter.

Address the cover letter directly

Often, applications don't have any information on who's posting the position. As such, addressing your cover letter to someone directly in the company is a nice touch. While doing so isn't always possible, you should strive to address the cover letter to the person in charge. You can call or email to get information on who posted the opening. In any event, addressing the letter to "Dear hiring or search committee," "Dear Sir or Madam," or "To Whom It May Concern" is an alternative to consider.

Avoid repeating your resume

A common mistake is merely copying and pasting from your resume. A cover letter is a storytelling to highlight specific items that make you the right person for the job. Otherwise, you may end up with a lengthy list of accomplishments without specific examples. Overall, your cover letter should elaborate a more detailed view of your accomplishments that could not be introduced fully on the resume.

Using a personal tone when necessary

An impersonal tone might make your letter seem like you didn't take the time to put a personal touch on it. In fact, it may seem like you're using a template. Thus, using a personal but professional tone will help you seem genuinely interested in the position. Don't be afraid to use personal pronouns such as "I," "me," or "my." However, don't overuse them. For example, starting every sentence with "I" might give an arrogant impression. Therefore, it's a good idea to use personal pronouns when necessary. This approach will make your cover letter look unique and authentic without seeming overly confident. Describing achievements such as "I improved sales by ten percent" may seem somewhat arrogant. Instead, stating this accomplishment as "My contributions helped the company improve sales by ten percent" makes this situation seem more like a team effort.

Only including relevant information

Like your resume, your cover letter should always remain relevant. For instance, if you've had various jobs, discussing the relevant jobs to your application is a must. Also, focusing on the studies and degrees that pertain to the application will help your application stand out. For example, if you're applying for a volunteer opportunity in a children's organization, highlighting your studies in political science may not necessarily boost your application. Instead, focusing on why you like working with children would make a much more compelling argument.

Keep it simple on one page

Please remember that time is a precious commodity. Application reviewers will not spend more than a few seconds to a couple of minutes on your cover letter. Thus, you must make your point in a one-page letter. This one-pager should highlight your motivation, reasons for applying, and why you're the right person for the job. Use your words and voice to reflect your personality. Great cover letters are generally short and sweet. Hopefully, that will pique the organization's interest so you can get that interview you want.

Double-check for spelling and grammar

Proofreading your letter is essential. After all, you only have one shot at a good first impression. Consequently, proofreading your letter will ensure that you avoid typos, grammatical errors, or misused terms. Additionally, please ensure that your cover letter matches your resume. The last thing you want is a discrepancy in the information you include in both the letter and resume.

Style is important

Style is a crucial element in a good cover letter. Please ensure you use an easily readable font (Georgia, Times New Roman, and Arial), a good size (12 points is the standard), and your spacing makes it easy to follow (1.5 spacing is the norm). Your letter might look crammed if you use a 10-point, single-spaced layout. This design may discourage a reviewer from going over your application. As a result, it's always a good idea to make your cover letter as easy to read as possible.

In most cases, your resume and cover letter will unlock the door to that coveted interview. Consequently, these tools must help highlight what you'll bring to the table if you are hired. Hopefully, these tools will get your foot in the door.

Now, let's look at how you can ace any interview when you get your chance.

ALL ABOUT INTERVIEWS

The predominant literature on interviews specifically focuses on job interviews. An interview doesn't necessarily need to be for a job. Often, volunteer organizations also interview their applicants before making a decision. Similarly, internships have rigorous application processes that include multiple interviews. As such, it is crucial for you to be ready for any interview situation.

American comedian Mitch Hedberg once quipped about job interviews with this zinger:

I had a job interview at an insurance company once, and the lady said, "Where do you see yourself in five years?" I said, "Celebrating the fifth-year anniversary of you asking me this question" (Crowley).

Indeed, being natural and authentic during an interview is important in creating a good first impression. After all, your interviewer is interested in what you bring to the team. The aim is to ensure you highlight who you truly are. That attitude is much more valuable than an inflated resume or "perfect" cover letter.

A common misconception is that interviews are an opportunity to "judge" applicants. Of course, interviewers use interviews to assess candidates. However, interviews are much more than simply "judging" candidates. Thus, let's look at the various purposes that interviews serve both interviewers and applicants.

PURPOSES OF AN INTERVIEW

An interview is an opportunity for everyone involved to gather information. It may be quite tough to gauge both the candidate and the opportunity without this meeting. Ultimately, a mismatch may occur.

Beyond information gathering, interviews serve various purposes:

Learn about each other

During an interview, both the organization and the candidate can learn about each other. The organization has a chance to learn more about the person interested in the role. The candidate can find out if this opportunity is right for them. For instance, a part-time job may look good on the surface. However, the schedule may clash with your class schedule. As such, the opportunity would not be the best fit.

Gauge the culture

Culture is a two-way street. For organizations, the cultures that sync with their values are crucial. Individuals need to determine if the organizational culture sits well with its objectives. For example, doing an internship with a company notorious for mistreating interns may not be your first choice. As such, you can determine if this organization's culture meshes with your specific needs.

Tell your story

An interview gives candidates the chance to tell their stories and highlight their achievements. After all, a cover letter and resume will only get interviewers' attention on you. Thus, organizations use interviews to hear more about a candidate's background. There is only so much a cover letter and resume can reveal. Therefore, organizations want to listen to your story, background, and specific examples of what you did in the past. It's much better to put a face to a resume than merely seeing black and white information in an application.

Relationship building

Interviews provide the first chance to build a relationship. Thus, you have an opportunity to connect with the organization and professionals right from the start. When you build rapport from the beginning, you have the chance to get off on the right foot. In contrast, a negative interview experience may serve as a red flag for everyone involved. Ultimately, you can build a relationship beyond the main professional or academic reasons. You can begin building a connection on a more personal level.

Discuss goals

Interviews clear the path to discuss goals and expectations. You can establish what you expect to achieve if given the opportunity. For example, you can explain how an internship would bolster your professional experience in the occupation. Moreover, you can explain how the opportunity contributes to your overarching career plan. Additionally, you can also determine if the chance will contribute to your goals meaningfully.

Indicate your value

Your full value isn't always apparent on a resume or cover letter. There are instances where your full value is noticeable until others meet you in person. Therefore, use an interview as a forum to indicate your value. Moreover, you can establish what value you bring to the table. In turn, you can determine what value the organization has for you as an individual. Ideally, both parties can build a symbiotic relationship that fosters individual and common objectives.

Don't forget to follow up once the interview is over. Sending a thank-you email is a great touch. A phone call can also work very well as a follow-up. Don't wait too long. Send a thank-you email right after the interview or the next day. Then, you can wait a few more days before touching base once again to follow up if you haven't heard from the interviewer. Please remember that it's the little things that make a significant difference in your career advancement.

ALL ABOUT LINKEDIN

LinkedIn is the premier professional and business social media platform in the world. According to LinkedIn, the network counts roughly 800 million users in over 200 countries ("About LinkedIn"). Thus, LinkedIn is a great source for building connections, establishing an online presence, and finding opportunities.

Please remember that LinkedIn is more than just an online resume or job board. While you can certainly get a job through LinkedIn, its purpose goes far beyond that.

Your main goal as a new college student should be to use LinkedIn to build your online presence. Recruiters, admissions officers, and professionals in general, will look you up on LinkedIn. A well-crafted professional profile speaks volumes about your personality. Otherwise, a sloppy profile will certainly send the wrong message.

Overall, your profile should reflect your skills and experience. It doesn't matter if you don't have much to include at this time. Take the time to include everything you feel is relevant to your profile carefully. For example, volunteering experiences, internships, awards, certificates, and training courses all help paint the portrait of who you are.

Please note that including relevant details about you is extremely important. You see, recruiters search for talent on LinkedIn using specific keywords. Your profile must present the keywords relevant to you and your career field. Doing so enhances your visibility.

Here are some great ideas you can implement to help you get the most out of your presence on LinkedIn:

- **Post interesting and share valuable content regularly.** Posting useful and relevant content to your contacts is a great way you can draw attention. Those around you will see that you're willing to share helpful information.
- **Join groups in your field.** LinkedIn has several groups you can join within your area. These groups often serve to network, share industry information, and support fellow members. Join as many groups as you can. Then, share

valuable content that helps others in your network.

- **Interact with others in your network**. No, I don't mean cold emailing others. You can make a name for yourself by commenting, sharing posts, and contributing to conversations. Eventually, your contributions will get your attention. Also, don't forget to send a thank-you message to anyone who adds you or accepts your request to connect.
- **Check out companies.** LinkedIn is a great place to research companies. You can learn a lot about a company or organization from their LinkedIn profile. So, follow companies and their top executives. Especially, focus on companies or organizations that belong to your specific domain. You never know when an interesting opportunity might pop up.
- **Engage recruiters.** Human resources professionals often peruse LinkedIn in search of talents. First, activate the "open to work" button. This feature notifies recruiters that you're open to opportunities. Next, interact with recruiters, human resources professionals, and admissions people. You can begin by establishing contact. From there, you can work your way up to your next opportunity.

148 | CAREER DEVELOPMENT FOR NEW COLLEGE STUDENTS

- **Apply.** Yes, you can always apply for jobs, internships, or even volunteer opportunities on LinkedIn. Suppose you already have contacts in that organization. In that case, LinkedIn will notify the poster that you are a part of their network. So, don't be afraid to apply online!

At the end of the day, LinkedIn is a tool you cannot ignore. If you aren't on LinkedIn, spend an hour or two on creating your profile. If you're already on LinkedIn, remember to keep updating it. Who knows, the opportunity you're looking for might be right around the corner.

TAKING THE OFFER

Congratulations! You have put together a solid effort leading you to the point where you need to decide and say "yes" to an offer put in front of you. Naturally, this decision is a serious matter. After all, making the wrong choice may cause you to lose precious time and possibly affect your academic performance. To help you in this process, here are some criteria to consider as you weigh your options:

- **Schedule**. Schedule plays a key role in your decision. Scheduling conflicts with your

current class load may negatively affect your
academic performance. Thus, you might
consider filling your weekends and summer
holidays with volunteer opportunities and
internships while focusing specifically on your
schoolwork during the regular semester.

- **Workload.** You must determine how
  demanding the opportunity may be. If it's too
  demanding, balancing a volunteer, job, or
  internship opportunity plus schoolwork may
  get overwhelming. So, it's best to start small
  and gradually build your way up.
- **Remote or online work.** If possible, working
  remotely may provide you with a chance to
  work in your chosen field. You can always do
  in-person work when it suits you best or when
  you can plan for it.
- **Relevance to your career field.** Naturally, any
  opportunity you accept must be relevant to
  your career field. Otherwise, you might want to
  pass.
- **Organizational culture.** It's crucial to ensure
  that the organization you choose to work with
  fits your personal interests and values. If these
  don't mesh, you might want to consider other
  options.
- **Recommendations.** Whenever possible, try to

get recommendations or referrals. If your peers, professors, or mentors recommend that you take an opportunity, go for it! If you're on the fence, but you have others cheering you on, take the plunge. Perhaps all you need is just a nudge in the right direction.

KEY TAKEAWAYS

Let's look at this chapter's key takeaways:

- Your CV or resume is a crucial tool to help you make a great first impression. As such, your CV or resume must be neat. Putting your best effort into your CV will help you stand out among your competition.
- A cover letter is your calling card. So, please ensure to personalize it for each application. Moreover, make sure your cover letter is tight and highlights the reasons why you are the best candidate for the position.
- Interviews are a great opportunity for all parties to get to know one another. Therefore, an interview will give you the chance to gauge an opportunity. On the flip side, organizations take these opportunities to meet you. They are not there to judge you. They are there to see if

you are a cultural fit. If all goes well, you could have the chance to begin a wonderful professional relationship.

- Take some time working on your LinkedIn profile and start making good use of the platform. Use it as a resource to explore the companies you want to work for, find the professional group and start building the connection. LinkedIn is not only a job postings site, but there are also rich resources and potential opportunities for you to discover.

- There are various elements to consider when deciding on the opportunity you wish to pursue. Above all, please ensure opportunities fit your values, interests, and goals. The last thing you want is to pursue an opportunity that doesn't contribute to your career exploration.

CONCLUSION

As we draw this conversation to a close, I recall the words of the late actor Chadwick Boseman, "Whatever you choose for a career path, remember the struggles along the way are only meant to shape you for your purpose" ("Remembering Actor Chadwick Boseman"). Indeed, these words resonate through the reality that we must encounter as we find our life's true purpose.

The struggles, challenges, and defeats we face are merely learning experiences. These experiences come with the territory. Of course, we would rather go through a straight path, free of any obstacles. But then again, wouldn't that make life too predictable?

There is no question that finding your true career path is an evolving matter. Whatever you uncover today may

not be the same tomorrow. Therefore, the most important thing to keep in mind is flexibility. As you traverse
through your professional life, please remember that
setbacks and obstacles may force you to change your
plans, but not your objectives.

At this point, I would like you to revisit the entire game
plan we have put together. I would like you to look at it
as a whole. You can see how the big picture can break
down into individual components when you do. Each
component is representative of a step in the journey.
However, it's also crucial to avoid losing focus. It's easy
for obstacles to sidetrack your progress.

When you feel you're losing focus, take a break. Often,
a break will help you recalibrate your focus. Things will
surely come back into focus as you reset your sights on
the target. As such, I'd like you to take time off whenever you can. Removing yourself from the situation
you're facing is a great way to catch your breath and
keep going.

It's okay to slow down sometimes. But it's never okay
to give up.

With that in mind, you might be thinking about what's
next. You are now ready to embark upon the personal
journey into career exploration. If you haven't
completed any of the exercises laid out in this book, I

strongly urge you to get started as soon as you can. You can start by crafting your objectives and career outlook. Most importantly, the aim is to visualize your dream career. From there, you can begin to break down the various steps along your path.

With your objectives in mind, it's time for your interests and values assessment. This assessment is critical in ensuring that your potential career options match your expectations. As such, taking any of the tests laid out in this book will help you get a clear picture of where you stand. Please remember that this is about what you want to achieve with your life. Therefore, you must be cognizant of what drives you. Thus, understanding your motivations will help you find the path that's right for you.

Next, I would like you to take some time out to consider the resources and information at your disposal. If possible, set aside a weekend, or a few weeknights, to do research on the various jobs out there. Please take this research seriously. After all, putting careful thought into this part of the process will save you plenty of time down the road.

As you map out what your career path looks like, you can begin to reach out to people who can help point you in the right direction. Take the time to write emails and make phone calls. Make time to pay personal visits and reach out to anyone you think might offer you support in your research. Eventually, your connection can help you test the waters in your chosen career field.

I know that this entire journey might seem like a lot to take in. However, the crucial thing is to start somewhere. If you never begin, you will never go anywhere. As the Buddhist adage goes, "The longest journey begins with a single step." Indeed, you must take that first today. The longer you put it off, the longer it will take you to reach your dream job.

Of course, finding that ideal job is a long and winding road. Your research might take you down an unexpected path. You may discover along the way that things aren't quite what you expected. That's perfectly fine! That's why we're here. We're here to eliminate the guesswork from your career path. It would be best if you saw what's out there for yourself. As you do, you can make the choices that are best for you.

What if you don't make the best choice?

It doesn't matter! Unlike other people out there, you have the luxury of time. You have the luxury of taking your time to do research and test water. Hopefully, you're not under pressure to take the first job that comes your way. You have the opportunity to build the career and the life of your dreams. That begins with that first. Your dream life begins today.

I want to thank you for taking the time to read this book. I hope it has provided you with insights that can help you make the right decision. Naturally, we all make mistakes, and the aim is to reduce those mistakes as much as possible.

If you feel this book has been useful and informative, please tell anyone you think will benefit from it. Who knows, you might be helping someone, just like you, build the career and life of their dreams. Thanks again.

LEAVE A 1 CLICK REVIEW

Did you enjoy the book? Please leave a review on Amazon. Your comments will help me to provide more valuable content!

Last but not least, I would like to offer you exclusive bonuses!

Bonus #1: you will be added to a Facebook group for career-related Q & A!

Bonus #2: you will receive a FREE career well-being assessment!

In addition, you have the opportunity to book a one-on-one 45 mins Need Assessment counseling session with me for FREE!

If you want to receive your bonus and personal career advice or career coaching, feel free to sign up at https://forms.gle/ZhiyF34a8QcgGTFB7. To be a part of your career success journey would be my honor! I will see you soon!

WORKS CITED

"20 Skills in Demand in Today's Workforce." *Indeed Career Guide,* www.indeed.com/career-advice/finding-a-job/in-demand-skills. Accessed 5 Aug. 2020.

"About LinkedIn." *About.linkedin.com,* about.linkedin.-com/#:~:text=Wel-come%20to%20LinkedIn%2C%20the%20world. Accessed 27 June 2021.

admin. *Yogi Berra – Society for American Baseball Research.* sabr.org/bioproj/person/yogi-berra/#:~:text=Many%20images%20come%20to%20mind.

"APA Dictionary of Psychology." *Dictionary.apa.org,* dictionary.apa.org/self-understanding. Accessed 28 Dec. 2021.

"Aptitude Testing over the Years." *Aptitude for Interpreting*, vol. 13, no. 1, 11 Apr. 2011, pp. 5–30, 10.1075/intp.13.1.02rus. Accessed 10 Sept. 2019.

Awaya, Allen, et al. "Mentoring as a Journey." *Teaching and Teacher Education*, vol. 19, no. 1, Jan. 2003, pp. 45–56, 10.1016/s0742-051x(02)00093-8. Accessed 15 Nov. 2019.

Bayl-Smith, Piers H., and Barbara Griffin. "Measuring Work Styles: Towards an Understanding of the Dynamic Components of the Theory of Work Adjustment." *Journal of Vocational Behavior*, vol. 90, Oct. 2015, pp. 132–144, 10.1016/j.jvb.2015.08.004. Accessed 5 Nov. 2019.

Ben-Shem, Idit, and Tamara E Avi-Itzhak. "On Work Values and Career Choice in Freshmen Students: The Case of Helping vs. Other Professions." *Journal of Vocational Behavior*, vol. 39, no. 3, Dec. 1991, pp. 369–379, 10.1016/0001-8791(91)90045-n. Accessed 11 May 2020.

Berra, Yogi. "Yogi Berra." *Baseball Hall of Fame*, baseball-hall.org/hall-of-famers/berra-yogi.

Brandon Reynolds. "Success Is Where Preparation and Opportunity Meet." *CREOnline*, 14 Aug. 2020, www.creonline.com/success-is-where-preparation-and-opportunity-meet/. Accessed 29 Dec. 2021.

Cambridge Dictionary. "CV | Meaning in the Cambridge English Dictionary." *Cambridge.org*, 9 Oct. 2019, dictionary.cambridge.org/dictionary/english/cv. Accessed 13 Oct. 2019.

---. "Resume." *@CambridgeWords*, 29 Dec. 2021, dictionary.cambridge.org/dictionary/english/resume? q=r%C3%A9sum%C3%A9. Accessed 29 Dec. 2021.

Chartrand, JM. *The Evolution of Trait-And-Factor Career Counseling: A Person× Environment Fit Approach.* 2021. Vol. 69(6):518-24, Journal of Counseling & Development, 8 July 1991.

Cohen, Alan. "Alan Cohen – Programs & Publications." *Www.alancohen.com*, www.alancohen.com. Accessed 29 Dec. 2021.

Cook, Alyssa F., et al. "The Prevalence of Medical Student Mistreatment and Its Association with Burnout." *Academic Medicine*, vol. 89, no. 5, May 2014, pp. 749–754, 10.1097/acm.0000000000000204. Accessed 21 May 2020.

Covey, Stephen R. "Stephen R. Covey – HABIT 2: BEGIN with the END in MIND." *Genius*, genius.com/Stephen-r-covey-habit-2-begin-with-the-end-in-mind-annotated. Accessed 29 Dec. 2021.

Crowley, James. "15 Classic Jokes to Remember Mitch Hedberg, 15 Years after His Death." *Newsweek*, 30 Mar. 2020, www.newsweek.com/mitch-hedberg-best-jokes-15th-anniversary-his-death-1493514. Accessed 30 Dec. 2021.

"Curriculum Vitae - Definition, What to Include, and How to Format." *Corporate Finance Institute*, corporatefinanceinstitute.com/resources/careers/resume/curriculum-vitae/. Accessed 5 Dec. 2020.

Dawis, Rene V. "Personnel Assesment from the Perspective of the Theory of Work Adjustment." *Public Personnel Management*, vol. 9, no. 4, July 1980, pp. 268–273, 10.1177/009102608000900406. Accessed 17 June 2019.

Dyrbye, Liselotte N., et al. "A Multicenter Study of Burnout, Depression, and Quality of Life in Minority and Nonminority US Medical Students." *Mayo Clinic Proceedings*, vol. 81, no. 11, Nov. 2006, pp. 1435–1442, 10.4065/81.11.1435. Accessed 25 May 2019.

"Employment and Unemployment among Youth Summary." *Bls.gov*, 2018, www.bls.gov/news.release/youth.nr0.htm. Accessed 28 Dec. 2021.

"Financial Managers: Occupational Outlook Handbook: : U.S. Bureau of Labor Statistics." *Bls.gov*, 13 Nov.

2018, www.bls.gov/ooh/management/financial-managers.htm. Accessed 1 Mar. 2019.

Forgues, S. *Aptitude Testing of Military Pilot Candidates.*

Garces-Jimenez, Mateo. "Covid Is Making College Students Rethink Their 'Dream Job' and Plans for after Graduation." *CNBC*, 3 Jan. 2021, www.cnbc.com/2021/01/03/covid-is-making-college-students-rethink-their-dream-job-.html. Accessed 18 Feb. 2021.

Gore, PA, and JL Hitch. *Occupational Classification and Sources of Occupational Information. Career Development and Counseling. Putting Theory and Research to Work.* . 2005, pp. 382–413. Accessed 29 Dec. 2021.

Harper, Melanie C., and Marie F. Shoffner. "Counseling for Continued Career Development after Retirement: An Application of the Theory of Work Adjustment." *The Career Development Quarterly*, vol. 52, no. 3, Mar. 2004, pp. 272–284, 10.1002/j.2161-0045.2004.tb00648.x. Accessed 23 Nov. 2019.

Jobs, Steve. "Text of Steve Jobs' Commencement Address (2005)." *Stanford News*, Stanford University, 14 June 2005, news.stanford.edu/2005/06/14/jobs-061505/.

Kagan, Julia. "How Cover Letters Work." *Investopedia*, www.investopedia.com/terms/c/cover-letter.asp. Accessed 30 Apr. 2020.

Kassem, Suzy. "Suzy Kassem Quotes." *Quoteslyfe*, www.quoteslyfe.com/quote/In-life-most-short-cuts-end-up-47676. Accessed 29 Dec. 2021

Kelly, Jack. "Recent College Graduates Confront Covid-19, Intense Competition and Three Years of Experience Required for an Entry-Level Job." *Forbes*, www.forbes.com/sites/jackkelly/2021/09/19/recent-college-graduates-confront-covid-intense-competition-and-three-years-of-experience-required-for-an-entry-level-job/?sh=6068edb37256. Accessed 29 Dec. 2021.

Kelly, Kevin R., and Heidi Jugovic. "Concurrent Validity of the Online Version of the Keirsey Temperament Sorter II." *Journal of Career Assessment*, vol. 9, no. 1, Feb. 2001, pp. 49–59, journals.sagepub.com/doi/abs/10.1177/106907270100900104, 10.1177/106907270100900104. Accessed 11 Dec. 2019.

Laker, Dennis R., and Jimmy L. Powell. "The Differences between Hard and Soft Skills and Their Relative Impact on Training Transfer." *Human Resource Develop-*

ment Quarterly, vol. 22, no. 1, Mar. 2011, pp. 111–122, 10.1002/hrdq.20063. Accessed 31 Jan. 2019.

Megginson, David. "Mentoring in Action: A Practical Guide (2nd Ed.)." *Human Resource Management International Digest*, vol. 14, no. 7, Dec. 2006, 10.1108/hrmid.2006.04414gae.002. Accessed 26 Jan. 2020.

Misner, Ivan. "Dr. Misner's Professional Blog." *Dr. Ivan Misner®*, ivanmisner.com. Accessed 29 Dec. 2021.

MLB. "Big Brothers Big Sisters New Sports Buddies Program Gets Big Endorsement from Area Athletes and Sports Teams." *Mlb.mlb.com*, mlb.mlb.com/content/printer_friendly/tb/y2008/m02/d18/c2378250.jsp. Accessed 29 Dec. 2021.

Oswald, Frederick, et al. *Stratifying Occupational Units by Specific Vocational Preparation (SVP)*. 1999.

Oswald, Gina R., et al. "Short-Term Job Shadowing Experience Benefits for Undergraduate Rehabilitation Students." *The Australian Journal of Rehabilitation Counselling*, vol. 23, no. 2, 13 Mar. 2017, pp. 79–89, 10.1017/jrc.2017.2. Accessed 4 June 2020.

Peterson, Jordan B. "'Don't Compare Yourself' | Jordan Peterson Motivation." *Www.youtube.com*, 22 Jan. 2021, www.youtube.com/watch?v=7dREKiDaA0c. Accessed 29 Dec. 2021.

philosiblog. "The Best Way to Predict the Future Is to Create It." *Philosiblog,* 17 May 2013, philosiblog.com/2013/05/17/the-best-way-to-predict-the-future-is-to-create-it/. Accessed 28 Dec. 2021.

"Remembering Actor Chadwick Boseman." *NPR.org,* 29 Sept. 2020, www.npr.org/2020/08/29/907512165/remembering-actor-chadwick-boseman. Accessed 30 Dec. 2021.

Robbins, Tony. "Tony Robbins - the Official Website of Tony Robbins." *Tonyrobbins.com,* www.tonyrobbins.com.

Robinson, Carrie H., and Nancy E. Betz. "A Psychometric Evaluation of Super's Work Values Inventory—Revised." *Journal of Career Assessment,* vol. 16, no. 4, 16 May 2008, pp. 456–473, 10.1177/1069072708318903. Accessed 3 June 2019.

Robles, Marcel M. "Executive Perceptions of the Top 10 Soft Skills Needed in Today's Workplace." *Business Communication Quarterly,* vol. 75, no. 4, 8 Oct. 2012, pp. 453–465, 10.1177/1080569912460400. Accessed 13 Mar. 2019.

Rodríguez, Carmen, et al. "Influence of Social Cognitive and Gender Variables on Technological Academic Interest among Spanish High-School Students: Testing Social Cognitive Career Theory." *International Journal for Educational and Vocational Guidance*, vol. 16, no. 3, 1 Sept. 2015, pp. 305–325, 10.1007/s10775-015-9312-8. Accessed 15 June 2019.

Rohm, RA. *What Is DISC. It Is a Powerful Way to Understand People and Their Personality Types*. 2013.

Schwartz, Nelson D., and Coral Murphy Marcos. "A Year after a Jobs Bust, College Students Find a Boom." *The New York Times*, 8 Oct. 2021, www.nytimes.com/2021/10/08/business/economy/college-graduates-jobs.html.

Snyderman, Mark, and Stanley Rothman. "Survey of Expert Opinion on Intelligence and Aptitude Testing." *American Psychologist*, vol. 42, no. 2, 1987, pp. 137–144, kodu.ut.ee/~spihlap/snyderman@rothman.pdf, 10.1037/0003-066x.42.2.137. Accessed 25 July 2020.

Stein, Randy, and Alexander B. Swan. "Evaluating the Validity of Myers-Briggs Type Indicator Theory: A Teaching Tool and Window into Intuitive Psychology." *Social and Personality Psychology Compass*, vol. 13, no. 2, 25 Jan. 2019, p. e12434, 10.1111/spc3.12434. Accessed 9 Nov. 2019.

Tokar, David M., and Jane L. Swanson. "Evaluation of the Correspondence between Holland'S Vocational Personality Typology and the Five-Factor Model of Personality." *Journal of Vocational Behavior*, vol. 46, no. 1, Feb. 1995, pp. 89–108, 10.1006/jvbe.1995.1006. Accessed 6 Oct. 2019.

Tracy, Brian. *Goals! : How to Get Everything You Want, Faster Than You Ever Thought Possible.* San Francisco, Berrett-Koehler Publishers, 2010.

Tyson, Mike. "https://Twitter.com/Miketyson/Status/1052665864401633299." *Twitter*, 27 Oct. 2018, twitter.com/miketyson/status/1052665864401633299? lang=en. Accessed 29 Dec. 2021.